Big Book of Weekend Beading

Big Book of Weekend Beading

CompanionHouse Books™ is an imprint of Fox Chapel Publishers International Ltd.

Project Team
Vice President–Content: Christopher Reggio
Editor: Anthony Regolino
Copy Editor: Laura Taylor
Design: Mary Ann Kahn
Index: Jay Kreider

ISBN 978-1-62008-282-9

Library of Congress Cataloging-in-Publication Data
Names: Cotgrove, Natalie, editor. | Power, Jean, editor.
Title: Big book of weekend beading / edited by Jean Power ; with
    contributions from Natalie Cotgrove, Umbreen Hafeez, Cheryl Owen, and
    Julie Smallwood.
Description: Mount Joy, PA : CompanionHouse Books, 2018. | Includes index.
Identifiers: LCCN 2017054448 | ISBN 9781620082829 (softcover)
Subjects: LCSH: Beadwork. | Bead embroidery.
Classification: LCC TT860 .B5496 2018 | DDC 745.594/2--dc23
LC record available at https://lccn.loc.gov/2017054448

This book has been published with the intent to provide accurate and authoritative information in regard to the subject matter within. While every precaution has been taken in the preparation of this book, the author and publisher expressly disclaim any responsibility for any errors, omissions, or adverse effects arising from the use or application of the information contained herein.

Fox Chapel Publishing
903 Square Street
Mount Joy, PA 17552

Fox Chapel Publishers International Ltd.
7 Danefield Road, Selsey (Chichester)
West Sussex PO20 9DA, U.K.

www.facebook.com/companionhousebooks

We are always looking for talented authors. To submit an idea, please send a brief inquiry to acquisitions@foxchapelpublishing.com.

Printed and bound in China
21 20 19 18   2 4 6 8 10 9 7 5 3 1

Big Book of Weekend Beading

Step-by-Step Instructions for 30+ Quick Beading Projects

Edited by Jean Power
With Contributions from Natalie Cotgrove,
Umbreen Hafeez, Cheryl Owen, and Julie Smallwood

Contents

Introduction ◈ 6

Materials, Tools, and Techniques ◈ 12

Quick Beading Projects

Introduction

Versatile, colorful, decorative, and glamorous—beads add sparkle and pizzazz to everyday items and make some exquisite pieces of jewelry.

It doesn't matter whether you're new to beading or whether you're already an experienced crafter, you'll be sure to find something here that's fun to make. It might be a piece of stylish jewelry, an embellished article of clothing, or a unique item for the home. Beautiful beads, gemstone chips, pearls, and crystals are a joy to work with, and this book contains projects ranging from a beaded throw to a decorated lamp shade, necklaces and charm bracelets, earrings and pendants. There are classic styles, such as a strand of pearls and embroidered napkins, and also more contemporary pieces, including a charm ring and a necklace created with Bali beads.

Four chapters cover all the main areas of beading: general beadwork, stringing, bead embroidery, and wirework. There are more than 30 projects featured in the book, and each chapter is designed to start you off with a few simple projects and then lead you on to more intricate work, always with full instructions on techniques and helpful step-by-step photographs.

A huge range of beads and materials is used, beginning with basic beading thread and wire and moving on to colored cord and ribbons, all chosen to set off the specific finish of the beads. You'll be amazed at the variety of looks you can achieve by using some simple findings, a selection of pretty beads, and a couple of basic tools.

Try combining different beads—such as glass beads, semiprecious stones, charms, shells, and sequins—to get a vibrant and unique effect, and use the project suggestions to create your own ideas by mixing colors, sizes, and textures.

All the essential techniques are thoroughly explained at the beginning of the book. The first chapter not only explains all the useful terminology used in the projects but it also has detailed instructions on such skills as how to begin and finish threading on beads, how to work with wire, using a loom, making a beaded fringe, and embroidering using beads. Make sure you read through this section first so that you have all the information you need to get started with these amazing projects.

Take advantage of the eclectic and gorgeous selection of beads that are readily available to you, and have fun adding a little sparkle to your home and accessories!

Materials, Tools, and Techniques

Beads

At the heart of all beadwork are the beads themselves. Beads are available in thousands of combinations of colors, sizes, materials, and designs. Whether made of glass, shell, stone, crystal, wood, paper, bone, or plastic, all it takes to make a bead is a hole you can take a thread through. Below are details on the most commonly available beads, all of which are featured in this book.

Shaped glass beads

Glass beads come in many different sizes and shapes: drops, cubes, rice-shaped, daggers, hearts, and squares to name a few. Bought individually or in mixed sets, they can be used to add texture and color to any project.

Cylinder beads

Cylinder beads fall under the same category as seed beads, but have straight sides and look like sections of tubing. Available in hundreds of colors, they are much more accurately sized than regular seed beads and are perfect if you want to have a uniform look to your work.

Pearls

Pearls are always popular in jewelry. They vary from glass and cultured to naturally grown, and are now available in many different sizes, colors, and shapes. As with semiprecious beads, pearls often have small holes, so take this into account when deciding how you want to use them or use a bead reamer to enlarge the holes.

Seed beads and rocailles

These are the small, colored glass beads used in bead stitches such as peyote or netting, as well as in stringing, wirework, or bead embroidery. Widely available, these beads come in a whole host of colors and are very versatile.

While seed beads are shaped like a doughnut, rocailles are taller, like small, rounder-edged cylinders. These beads vary in size and are numbered accordingly. Confusingly, the smaller the number, the larger the bead. If you are looking for a large bead for stringing or for bolder projects, go for a size 8 or 6. If, on the other hand, you are looking for small beads for embroidery or delicate projects, go for a size 14 or 15. The most widely available size and the one most commonly used in beadwork is size 11, but use sizes 9 or 10 if this is what you have available.

Bugle beads

Bugle beads are long, thin tubes of glass. They come in many different lengths, colors, and finishes. While they look beautiful in your work, be aware that they have sharp edges, which may cut your thread.

Crystals and fire-polished beads

Crystal beads add sparkle and color to bead- and wirework. Whether small or large, crystals have a unique look and finish. They vary in price, depending on the quality of workmanship, with Austrian

Beads

Cylinder beads

Semiprecious beads

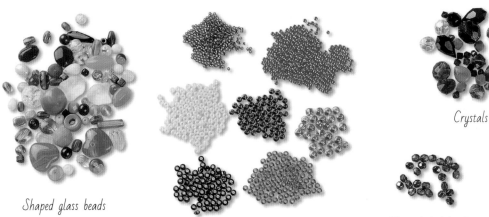

Shaped glass beads

Seed beads and rocailles

Crystals

Fire-polished beads

Cylinder beads

Bugle beads

Pearls

Beads

Lampwork beads

Metal beads and charms

Magnetic beads

Shells

Sequins

Sequins

Wooden beads

Sequins

Sequins

crystals being the most expensive. These crystals have the sharpest cut and finish and therefore the most sparkle and dazzle. Use them sparingly to add highlights and shots of color and shine.

Fire-polished (FP) beads are more affordable glass beads that can be used to add just as much sparkle and color for a fraction of the price.

Semiprecious beads

Available in thousands of different stones, cuts, colors, and sizes, from small chips to large chunks, with every size and shape in between, semiprecious beads always add a special touch to a piece.

Lampwork beads

Lampwork beads are handmade beads that can be one of a kind or made in sets. Each bead is made by hand, so this is reflected in the price. Used carefully, however, they can add an extra touch to your work that is worth the price.

Metal beads and charms

Metal beads and charms are becoming much more popular and come from all over the world. Whether from Thailand, India, Bali, or elsewhere, the quality of the work is reflected in the price.

Magnetic beads

These beads stick to each other as if by magic. Try simply stringing a single long strand, mixed with other beads, on flexible beading wire that you can then wrap around your wrist for a changeable and easily removed bracelet.

Shells

Shell beads add an exotic touch to your work, which regular glass beads may not. Available as whole shells or chips, they can also be purchased in their natural state or dyed for a different look.

Wooden beads

Available in a range of sizes, wooden beads vary from unfinished (ready for decorating or painting) to fully finished (polished, beautiful exotic woods) and add a natural look to your work. Wooden beads usually have large holes so that they can be easily threaded onto cord.

Sequins

Although not beads as such, sequins combine wonderfully with beads when used in embroidery. Usually made of plastic, but occasionally of metal, sequins come in a wide range of colors and shapes. Round sequins are flat- or cup-shaped, and the cups can be used right side up to reflect light in different ways. Whether sewn on individually or in groups, sequins are sure to add color and texture to your work. As with all beads, check the sequins for colorfastness before you add them to a piece that may need to be washed.

Crafter's Tip

Beads come in a variety of finishes, some of which are more permanent than others. Glass, pearls, and semiprecious beads can be dyed, an effect that may last but can also come off with wear. If you are unsure about a finish or want to use a bead in a piece that may be worn or washed frequently, it is a good idea to test the colorfastness.

To do this, simply place the beads in warm water and see if they discolor. To see if they stand up to washing, wash them with detergent. Alternatively, soak them in nail polish remover or bleach to see if the finish changes. It is advisable to let your beads dry on a white fabric or tissue to see more clearly if any color runs.

Threads, Wires, and Stringing Materials

Threads and wires are the materials that hold your beading projects together. Varying from fine and delicate threads to thick and strong wires, you will need to make sure you choose the appropriate material for your project.

Beading thread

Beading threads are available from any bead store. These come in a variety of colors and are perfect for beading stitches such as peyote or netting. Made of nylon, they stand up well to use, and you can choose a color that will complement your work or a neutral color that will blend into your project. Some colors may run, however, and you may find that your hands become discolored while working. If you want to use a beading thread in a piece of embroidery that may be washed or you don't want the color to run onto the fabric, it is always best to test it for colorfastness as you would beads.

Embroidery thread

If you are doing bead embroidery, you may choose to use embroidery thread instead of beading thread. Available in a much wider range of colors than beading thread, this is good for embroidery because the thread can sometimes show. Embroidery threads are also mainly colorfast and suitable for washing, but check the labels to make sure. These threads are available in cotton or silk and can be purchased in different finishes, such as metallic, which means that the thread can be just as much of a feature as the beads or sequins.

Threads, Wires, and Stringing Materials

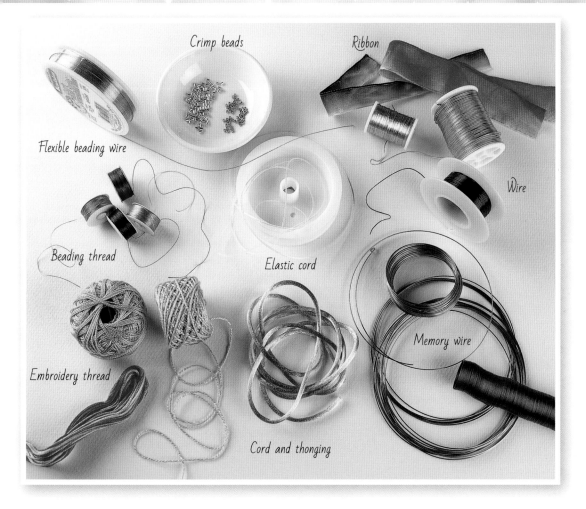

Crimp beads

Ribbon

Flexible beading wire

Wire

Beading thread

Elastic cord

Embroidery thread

Memory wire

Cord and thonging

Flexible beading wire

This strong yet flexible wire is perfect for stringing projects, especially those using heavy beads or those with potentially sharp edges. Unlike regular wire, this specialized product is made up of many fine strands of stainless steel, coated with nylon. The use of many strands is what gives it its strength but still allows it to remain flexible, like a thread or cord. Since this wire does not hold a knot, however, it needs to be finished using crimp beads.

Crimp beads

These are small metal beads designed to be squashed with pliers. They are used to secure flexible beading wire because their metal edges, when crimped, bite into the nylon coating, creating a secure finish. When crimped using specialized crimping pliers, you can form a more rounded end result; using flat-nose pliers will result in a flat, squared crimp.

Threads, Wires, and Stringing Materials

Elastic cord

Elastic cord is perfect for making quick jewelry items. Designed to be stretched, it can be used to make all-in-one pieces of jewelry without the need for clasps or fastenings. However, the cord must be knotted in a certain way to prevent it from unraveling (see the Techniques section on page 38).

Cord and thonging

When stringing beads, you can use various types of cord and thonging—leather, hemp, cotton, or rubber. All you need to be sure of is that it will comfortably fit through the hole in the beads. There is a fabric cord called rattail, which is made from satin and comes in a small range of colors. Available in different widths, this cord is ideal for making jewelry and looks good when knotted between beads.

Ribbon

Ribbon comes is so many different widths, colors, fabrics, textures, and designs that once you start incorporating it into your work, you'll find it a useful material to add interest and texture.

Wire

Wire comes in many colors and gauges (thicknesses). When making jewelry, a 20-gauge or 0.8-mm wire is perfect to work with, but depending on what you are making and what beads you are working with, you may like the look of a larger or smaller gauge. The wire you choose can vary from gold or silver to colored craft wires. Choose whichever wire you feel suits your project best.

Memory wire

This wire has been specially toughened so that it keeps its shape, no matter how much you pull, twist, or bend it—hence its name. Available in ring, bracelet, and necklace sizes, it can be used to make quick bead jewelry. Because the wire is tougher than other wires, you will not be able to use regular wire cutters when working with it, so special memory wire cutters are available. To finish a piece made of memory wire, simply turn the ends using round-nose pliers to create loops that will keep the beads from falling off.

Findings

Findings are those little bits that are essential to finishing beading or jewelry projects. In this book the findings used include clasps, jump rings, earring fittings, end caps, and head pins, but there are many more. The findings you choose depend on what you are making, the look you like, the size you need, or even just which metal you prefer.

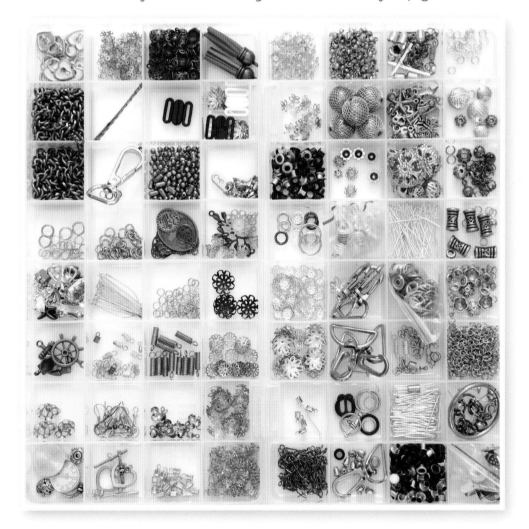

Findings

Earring findings

Many different earring findings are available, from small studs and posts to large chandelier fittings. What size and style you choose will depend on what look you want to achieve. When making a bead earring, you may choose a small finding that doesn't detract from your beadwork, or you may choose to make a feature of the finding. The only requirement for a fitting to attach beadwork to is that it has a small loop or open section on it to which you can attach your bead or wirework. Some findings will need to be opened with pliers, and some you can simply thread onto your beadwork as you bead. Other earring findings are designed for ears that are not pierced, and you attach your work in the same way.

Clasps

The variety of clasps available is huge. Clasps vary from small trigger clasps to toggles, box catches, magnetic catches, or s-hooks, with many different styles in between. Choose a clasp that suits your work in size, design, or color and make sure it is one you are comfortable using, especially on necklaces you may have to fasten without seeing what you're doing or on bracelets where you may be fastening them with one hand.

Jump rings

Jump rings are small metal rings that are essential when joining segments of wirework or attaching beadwork to findings. Available in many different sizes, wire gauges, and metals, these rings take a lot of the strain in a piece of jewelry, and it is therefore important to choose ones that are easy to open when you want to and ones that will stay closed when necessary. You can also use jump rings to make your own chain for bracelets or necklaces.

Findings

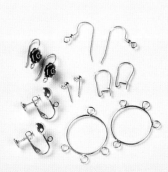

Earring findings

Clasps

Jump rings

Eyeglass findings

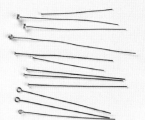

Head pins and eye pins

Cord endings

Calottes

End caps and cones

Key ring findings

Findings

Eyeglass findings

These findings are used for attaching bead- or wirework to your glasses to form attractive and useful chains. Available in different finishes and materials, choose a pair that will complement your design.

Head pins and eye pins

These small lengths of wire are used for making charms or dangles. Whereas head pins have a small flat or decorated section at one end on which to hold your bead, eye pins have a loop. After threading a pin or groups of beads onto either, you can make a loop at the other end and have an instant charm or dangle to add to your work.

Calottes

These are small findings that cover knots at the end of a thread or cord and help you attach the work to a clasp or other finding. Available in different sizes and choices of metal, these can also be called bead tips or necklace endings.

Cord endings

These metal findings come in many variations, but all have the use of finishing off the end of your cord. Some have clasps attached, but many just have a ring onto which you add the clasp of your choice.

End caps and cones

These are designed to cover the end of stringing materials in a finished piece of jewelry. Small semicircles are called end caps, and longer ones are called cones. They can be elaborate or plain and are usually made of silver, although they can be found in other metals.

Key ring findings

These are large metal rings on which you can attach some bead- or wirework. They can also have chains on them, which you can further embellish if you wish.

Tools

Wire-working tools come in a variety of styles, makes, and price ranges. When you first start out, however, a few simple tools are all that you need to create beautiful jewelry. Choose tools that fit comfortably in your hands and that aren't too big, small, or heavy for you.

Scissors (1)
When doing any beading or embroidery, it's always best to use fine scissors. Never use fine scissors for cutting paper, because it will blunt them, and never use them for cutting wire, especially memory wire.

Needles (2)
Beading needles come in a variety of lengths, but one thing they have in common is their fineness. Choose a needle that feels comfortable to work with and that will fit through the beads you are using without any difficulty.

Bead board (3)
If you plan on doing a lot of stringing, a bead board may be a worthwhile investment. These boards have grooves in which to place beads and plan out your designs. You can move the beads around until you achieve a design you are happy with before stringing. With measurements running alongside the grooves and storage compartments to safely hold your beads, a bead board can be an invaluable accessory.

Glue or clear nail polish (4)
Glue and nail polish can be useful when making jewelry. Either can be used to stiffen cord ends, and superglue can be used to secure knots in elastic cord.

Tools

File (5)

You can purchase files especially for filing wire, which will give you a professional, neat finish. If you don't have any on hand, you can use an emery board or metal nail file instead.

Bead reamers (6)

These specially designed files are used to file away the inside of a bead hole to make it larger if necessary. Wet the file with water before filing and keep it wet to avoid its getting clogged with dust as you're using it.

Loom (7)

Looms come in many sizes and makes. You want to buy one that is long and wide enough to hold the sort of items you'd like to make (i.e., long enough to fit a full-length bracelet).

Wire cutters (8)

Some cutters will make a notable difference depending on which way around they are used. Pay attention to what side of the blade gives you the best and smoothest finish and aim to use this side when cutting wire. Do not use standard wire cutters to cut memory wire, as this is made from a much tougher metal that will permanently damage standard wire cutters.

Memory wire cutters (9)

These are much stronger than standard wire cutters and are designed to cope with the tough metal used in memory wire.

Round-nose pliers (10)

Both jaws of these pliers are rounded. These pliers are used for making loops on wire.

Flat-nose pliers (11)

Flat-nose pliers are perfect for making bends, opening and closing rings and findings, and generally holding your work.

Chain- or needle-nose pliers (12)

These pliers have flat jaws that taper toward the tips. They are perfect for more delicate work or for getting into smaller spaces that flat-nose pliers can't reach.

Crimping pliers (13)

As their name suggests, these pliers are used for crimping beads. They create a neater, more rounded crimp that works well on strung necklaces. They are also useful for finishing off wrapped loops because their rounded sections help to push in the ends of the wire.

Large, blunt needle or awl (14)

Used for creating holes in fabrics without using something with a sharp point. You can also use a blunt needle or awl when knotting to slide knots up close to the beads.

Ring mandrel (15)

These cylindrical tools are made of wood or metal and are ideal for making perfect-sized rings. They come plain or with markings indicating different ring sizes. Simply place a ring you already own over the mandrel to check the size. If you can't get hold of a mandrel,

Crafter's tips

Tracing paper or baking parchment is perfect to use for copying designs so that you can transfer them onto your chosen fabric.

When you are beading, it is best to use a **bead mat** or other nonslip surface to make sure the beads don't roll off your work surface.

any cylindrical object of the right size can be used, such as a wooden dowel or a large pen.

Embroidery hoop (16)

This is a useful accessory when doing bead embroidery. The hoop is designed to hold any fabric on which you are beading taut so that the work stays neat and regular.

Design-transfer paper (17)

This specially coated paper is designed for transferring patterns and motifs onto fabric. Available in a variety of colors to ensure it shows up on even the darkest of fabrics, you use it by taping it, colored side down, onto fabric and drawing or tracing over it. Do not use pins to hold it down, because they can cause some of the color to transfer onto the fabric.

General Beading Techniques

Beadwork involves using different stitches to join beads together with the help of just a needle and thread. Each stitch produces a particular effect, but the stitches can be varied and used together to create an endless array of beautiful projects.

Stop bead

A stop bead is a bead that is added to the start of the thread to stop the rest of the beads from falling off the end. This bead is removed when you have finished the work.

1 | To add a stop bead, take the needle and thread through a bead at least twice.

2 | Make sure you don't pierce the thread with the needle, because this will make it harder to remove without damaging the thread. When you have finished the work, or no longer need the stop bead, pull off to remove.

Starting and ending thread

In beadwork, you should minimize the number of knots you make because they may show in the work. When you start or finish the thread, weave it through the beadwork so that it is secure and then trim it as close to the work as possible.

1 | It is always best to weave the end of the thread through the work so it crosses itself and can't work itself loose.

2 | Start the thread in the same way by weaving through the work until you get to where you last finished, then carry on beading.

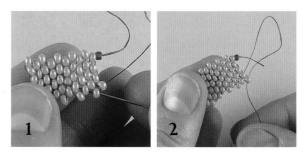

General Beading Techniques

Peyote stitch

Peyote stitch is one of the oldest beading stitches, and it is used for many different items. Once you have started the stitch, you then simply add beads into the gaps created. The samples below use different-colored beads for each step so you can follow the various stages with ease.

1 | Thread on a stop bead, if using; then pick up an even number of beads the width you would like the finished work to be. These beads will form the first and second rows. Two different-colored beads are used here, so even though the beads are threaded on together, they will form two separate rows.

2 | To start the third row, pick up a new bead and, skipping the last bead you picked up, turn and take the needle and thread through the next bead.

3 | Pick up another bead and, skipping the next bead—the third from the end—take the needle and thread through the next bead, which is the fourth.

4 | Continue picking up and adding beads, making sure you miss every other bead you originally threaded on until you reach the end of the third row. The work may begin to curve, but the more rows you add, the straighter it will get.

5 | To start the fourth row, pick up one bead, turn, and go through the last bead in the third row. By now you should see that the beads added at the beginning have shifted so that every other bead lies lower down. This creates the gaps into which all subsequent beads will be added. Continue adding beads into each gap until you reach the end of the row.

6 | Continue in this way until the work is the length you require; then weave the thread through the work to secure and finish.

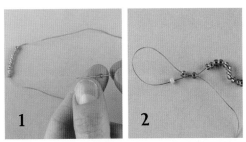

1

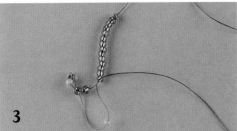

2

3

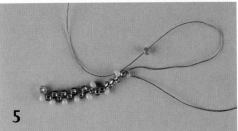

4

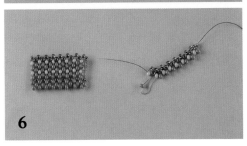

5

6

General Beading Techniques

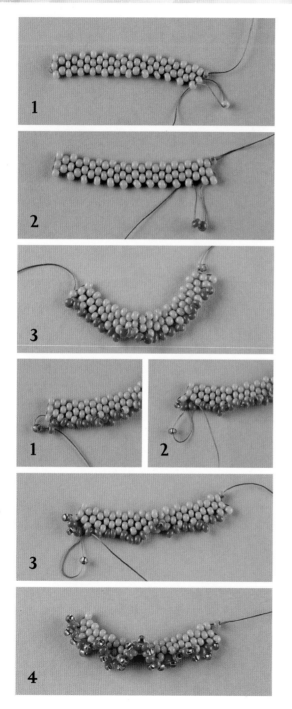

Increasing in peyote stitch

When beading the peyote stitch, you can add extra beads into each space: This is called increasing. You can do this to make something larger by giving each row more stitches, or to add more texture to the work, because these extra beads tend to distort the work, making it "frill."

The increasing row

1 | Take the needle and thread through the bead ahead of where you want to increase or frill your work.

2 | Pick up 2 beads instead of 1 bead and go through the next one as you would normally.

3 | Continue beading, adding 2 beads into each space. Because you are trying to fit twice the number of beads that will fit comfortably into each space, they will start to frill.

Subsequent rows

When you get back to where you previously increased, you need to separate the beads you added by placing a bead in between them.

1 | Add the last bead before reaching the increase. Take the needle and thread through a red bead, thread on a pink bead, then pass through a red bead again.

2 | Pick up 1 bead and go through the second increasing bead.

3 | Add a bead between each of the beads in the increase row.

4 | Continue adding beads. The more increasing you do, the bigger or frillier the work will become.

General Beading Techniques

Netting

Netting stitch is very similar to peyote stitch, but the number of beads you add each time and the number of beads you miss each time vary. There are two forms of netting—horizontal (left) and vertical (right).

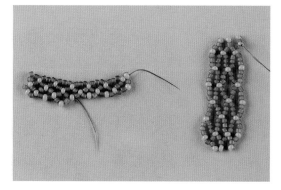

Horizontal netting

Horizontal netting is when you work from left to right.

Vertical netting

Vertical netting is when you work from top to bottom.

Stepping up at the start of the row

When beading some stitches, such as peyote or netting, you may find that you need to "step up" to begin a new row. "Stepping up" means weaving through the work to make sure you are in the correct position to start a new row. This occurs when you are beading these stitches as continuous circles. As you finish each row, work the needle and thread through the work so you are in the correct position to start the next row.

In peyote stitch

1 | Add the last bead in the row. Take the needle and thread up through the first bead in this row.

2 | You are now in the right position to add the first bead of the next row.

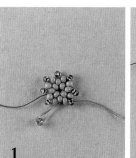

In netting

1 | Add the loop or group of beads for that row. Take the needle and thread up through the first loop of beads in that row, and exit out of the central bead or beads.

2 | You are now in the correct position to add the first loop or group of beads for the next row.

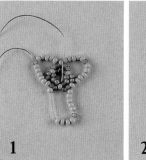

General Beading Techniques

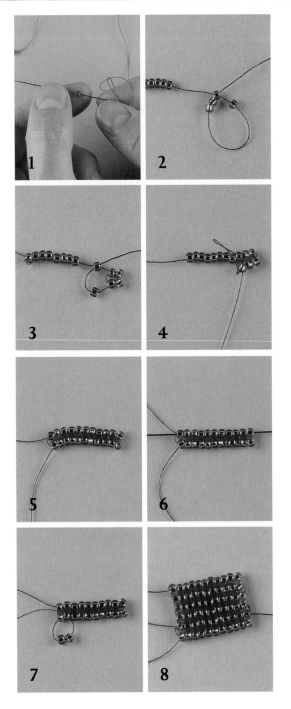

Square stitch

Not everyone likes to do loom work, so the square stitch may be a good alternative. You don't need a loom with square stitch, and there are no warp threads to deal with. This is a good, strong stitch, and it is surprisingly simple to learn.

1 | To begin, string a row of beads. The number of beads strung depends on how wide you want the finished item to be.

2 | For the second row, string on 2 more beads and pass the needle through the second-to-last bead of the first row, then back through the second of the 2 beads just strung.

3 | String another bead onto the thread and then pass through the third-to-last bead of the first row.

4 | Go through the third bead of the second row—that is, the last bead you have just strung.

5 | Repeat Step 4 to finish the second row.

6 | Once you get to the end of the second row, pass the needle and thread through all the beads of the first row. Then continue to pass the needle and thread through the last row just added.

7 | To start the third row, string 2 beads and repeat Step 2, using the 2 beads from the second row instead of the first row. Repeat until the item has reached the desired length.

8 | To finish, weave the thread back through the previous rows, tying knots between the beads at intervals until the work is secure.

General Beading Techniques

Loom work

The threads strung on a loom are called warp threads. The number of warp threads you need will depend on the number of beads you are using. You will always need to string one more warp thread than the number of beads used.

    Note: Repeat the steps on the next groove of each rod until you have 1 warp thread more than the number of beads in the widest row in your design (9 beads across = 10 warp threads).

    Make sure the threads are of equal tension. If they twang, they are wound on too tightly; if they slump unevenly, they are too loose. Make any adjustments before tying off the thread around a peg. You can run wax up and down the warp threads to strengthen them if desired.

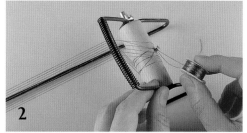

Setting up the loom

1 | To begin, knot the warp threads over a fixed peg.

2 | Hold the spool, allowing a steady feed of thread. Thread into a groove and continue unspooling across the loom; then thread into the corresponding groove at the other end. Wrap the thread around the peg at that end.

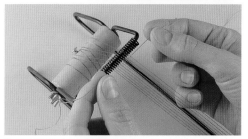

Starting off

Cut a length of thread 24–26 in. (60–66 cm) long. Tie the thread to the outside warp.

    Note: Tie onto the left warp if you are right-handed and vice versa.

Adding rows

1 | String on the first row of beads and bring them under the warp threads. Slide the beads toward the knot you just tied.

2 | Hold the beads in place (1 bead between each 2 warp threads) and push them up. Pass the weft thread back through the beads, but go over the warp threads this time. Keep adding rows in this way.

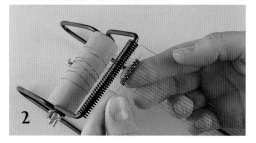

General Beading Techniques

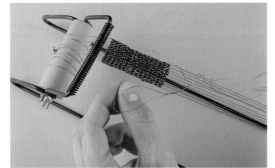

Adding a new thread

When adding a new length of thread to the weft thread (the thread that runs perpendicular to the warp threads), start by passing the thread through a previously added row, knotting between beads a couple of times. Weave up and down some of the previous rows before starting a new row.

Finishing a thread

Make sure you have plenty of thread to finish the row you have started and then some. Once you have finished a row, weave back through the beadwork, tying knots between random beads. Cut off the remaining thread.

Finishing off work

1 | Remove the wooden spools from the loom and unwind the warp threads from around them.

2 | If the threads are very long, cut them a little, but make sure you have enough to finish the piece.

3 | Weave each thread back into the beadwork and bring them out near the center of the first row.

4 | When all the threads are in position, tie a knot and finish off with a calotte. Repeat on the other side.

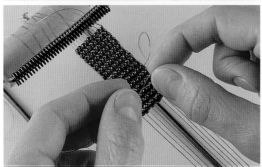

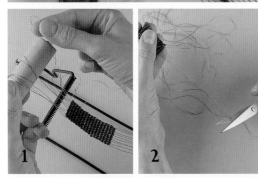

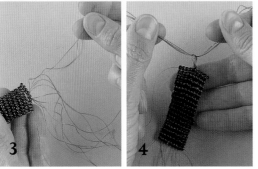

General Beading Techniques

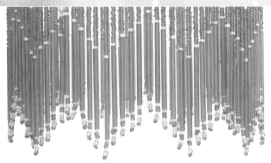

Fringing

Fringing refers to strands of beads that can be added to the edge or surface of items in order to embellish them.

1 | Secure a thread to the surface to which you are adding a fringe. Coming out at the front of the surface or fabric, pick up the length of beads you want as the fringe.

2 | Skipping the last bead, take the needle and thread up through the rest of the strand, then back into the work.

3 | Pull the fringe to tighten it, but make sure you leave a little slack so that the fringe can move and sway freely. Continue adding fringe until you have covered the surface or edge of the item.

Transform a plain lamp shade with an attractive beaded fringe.

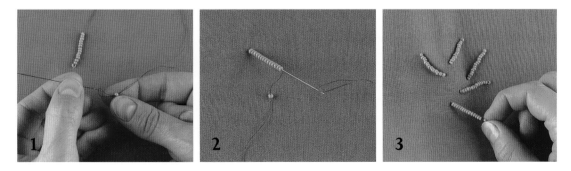

Stringing Techniques

Stringing means arranging strands of beads onto a stringing material. You can use beading wire, thread, elastic, or cord to create the perfect project. Space beads with knots or combine beads to create a piece of jewelry that suits your taste.

Stringing

It is worth planning your project before you begin to string it to save time later if you decide it doesn't look right.

1 | Lay the beads out on a bead board or other suitable surface. Arrange the beads until you find a combination you like.

2 | Begin stringing the beads on your chosen stringing material. It is best to start from the middle outward to be sure each side matches. This also makes it easier to make any changes as you go along. When you are satisfied with the design, finish both ends and attach a fastening.

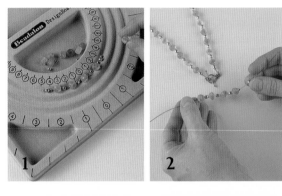

Crimping

Crimping is essential when working with flexible beading wire because this type of wire cannot be knotted. You can either use flat-nose pliers or crimping pliers; each will give different results.

For a more rounded look: Use crimping pliers (left).

For a flat, square look: Use flat-nose pliers (right).

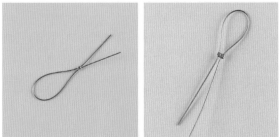

Crafter's Tip

When doing any crimping, gently pull the work to make sure the crimps have bitten into the wire coating enough to hold. Do not tug the work: if the crimps haven't held, the beads may scatter everywhere!

Stringing Techniques

Using crimping pliers

These pliers have 2 sections that you use, in turn, to create the finished crimp.

1 | First place the crimp bead, with the flexible beading wire inside, into the notched section closest to the handles of the pliers. Make sure the wires are separated and press the pliers to squash the crimp.

2 | Place the crimp into the other notched section, with the wires lying above one another, and press the pliers to fold the crimp and make it more rounded. You can move the crimp in the notch and press the pliers again if you feel it could be more rounded.

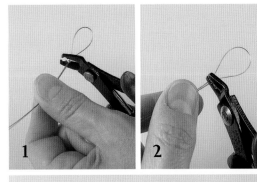

Using flat-nose pliers

Flat-nose pliers have jaws that are flat, straight-sided lengths of metal.

Simply place the crimp-covered wires into the jaws of the flat-nose pliers and press gently to squash the crimp.

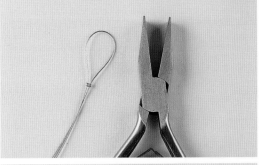

Gluing cord ends to get them through beads

When buying threading cord made of leather, suede, fabric, or any material thicker than string, always make sure it fits through the holes of the beads you want to use. Bead holes can be quite small, so it's always best to check. If you have any difficulty threading the cord, you may need to create your own "needle."

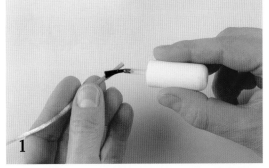

1 | Coat the end of the cord, at least 1 in. (2.5 cm), with PVA glue or clear nail polish and set aside to dry.

2 | When dry, cut the end of the cord at a 45-degree angle to create a point. The end should go through the beads with ease and can be trimmed off when you have finished.

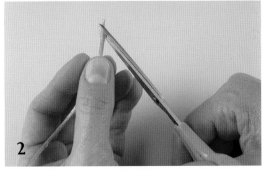

Stringing Techniques

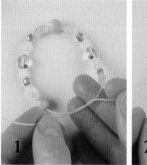

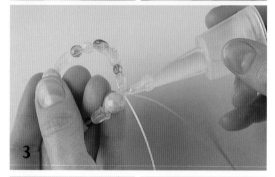

Ending elastic cord

Clear elastic cord must be ended with a square knot and superglued to make sure it holds. When you are tying the knot, stretch the cord slightly so there will be no gaps when you're done. Always tie the knot as close as possible to the beads.

1 | Lay the work with the cord ends facing you. Put the right end over the left and pull it through the center.

2 | Put the cord end, which is now on the left, over the right and pull it through the center of the knot.

3 | Place a dot of superglue onto the knot and let dry; then trim the cord ends and pull the cord so the knot sits inside one of the bead holes.

Making a wire needle

When working with ribbon, or other thick stringing material such as cord, you may find it tricky to thread it through the eye of the needle or even through the bead. What you can do is make a needle out of wire.

1 | Cut a 3-in. (7.5-cm) length of very fine wire. Fold the wire in half and twist the ends together, making sure to leave a small loop at the bend to act as the eye of the needle.

2 | Thread the end of the ribbon through the eye of the wire needle and use it in the same way as you would a needle.

3 | You can also pierce the ribbon with the wire before you begin twisting it because this reduces the bulk of ribbon you are trying to thread.

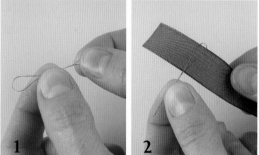

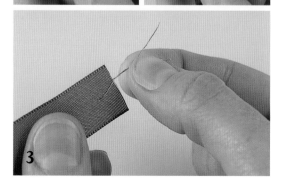

Stringing Techniques

Knotting

Knotting between beads means tying knots between the beads in the stringing material. It has three main purposes:

- It frames each bead so that the individual beads stand out more.
- It was originally done with pearls so that if the cord or thread broke, you would lose only 1 pearl and not the whole strand.
- It can be used to make a few beads go a long way.

Note: When you are knotting, make sure you are happy with where the knots are before tightening them; otherwise, it may be impossible to undo them.

1 | Work out your design and plan where you want the beads and knots to be placed. You can either sketch out your design or place the beads on a bead board until you achieve the perfect design.

2 | When threading the beads onto the cord or thread, it is best to start at one end and thread the beads on one at a time. Knots use up a lot of cord, so allow cord that is at least three times the length of the finished item.

3 | Lay the cord out in front of you. The beads and cord need to be loose so that you can adjust everything as you go along. Lay one end of the cord over the other to create a loop.

4 | Pull the end of the cord that lies on top through the loop from the back to the front. Make sure not to tighten it yet and leave it quite loose.

5 | To start tightening the knot, place a blunt needle or awl in the middle of the knot to guide it along the cord to the right place, near the bead.

6 | When the knot is close to the bead, take out the needle or awl and pull the knot tight. Keep adding beads and knots until your design is complete.

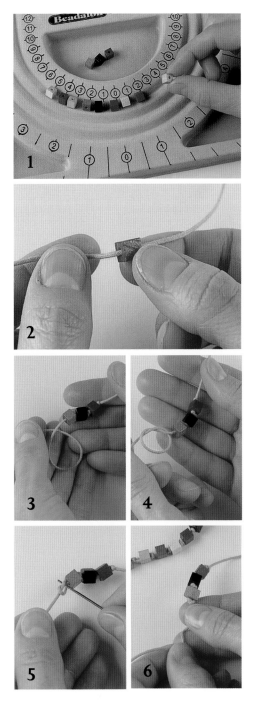

Stringing Techniques

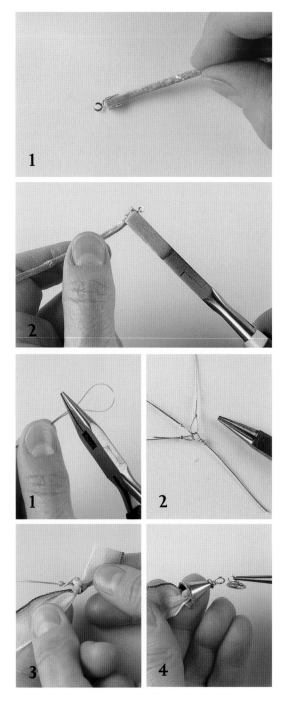

Using cord findings

Cord findings are used to finish off the ends of the cord and help you attach a clasp if you want.

1 | Coat the ends of the cord in glue or clear nail polish if you think the cord is likely to fray. When dry, place the cord end into the finding. Push it in as much as possible so it cannot be pulled out easily.

2 | If the cord ending has two sides to fold in, press these in one at a time as much as possible with flat-nose pliers to bite into the cord and hold it.

Using end caps or cones

Using end caps is an effective way to hide messy ends on your work. Make sure you read through these instructions carefully, because what you have strung the beads on will affect how you join the strands.

1 | If you are using flexible beading wire to string on the beads, make sure you create a loop at each end; then crimp to secure.

2 | If the strands are on flexible beading wire, make sure you go through all the end loops before creating the wrapped loop.

3 | If some of the strands are ribbon or cord, knot all the ends together through the loop on the wrapped loop.

4 | Put the wire end through the end cap or cone. Finish the end of the wire by creating a turned or wrapped loop, and attach it to the clasp.

Stringing Techniques

Using calottes

Also called necklace ends, calottes sit over knots or beads at the end of the thread and join the work onto a clasp. They protect the thread from rubbing against the metal of a clasp and fraying. Calottes can be used with flexible beading wire, thread, cord, or any other threading material that can be knotted.

1 | Tie an overhand knot in the thread and, if using more than one thread, knot them together. Do this as close to the beadwork as possible, but make sure there is a gap of at least 1/16 in. (1 mm) between the beads and the knot. Do not cut the ends of the thread yet.

2 | Add a dab of glue or clear nail polish into the open calotte; this will help you place the knot and hold it secure when trimming the ends.

3 | Place the knot into the open calotte. If there is a notch in the side of the calotte, rest the threads into this. Trim the threads, making sure the knot doesn't fall out of the calotte.

4 | With the flat-nose pliers, gently close up the calotte until it shuts as much as possible.

5 | Gently pull the calotte to check that it has held; then using the hook or loop on the calotte, attach the clasp.

6 | If you are using only one thread, you can thread on a bead, place this in the calotte, then weave the needle and thread back into the work to secure.

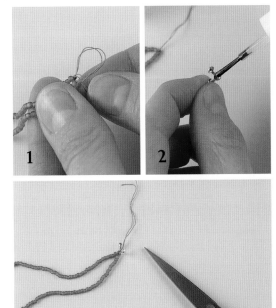

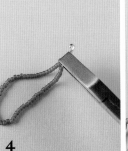

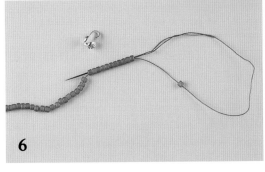

Bead Embroidery Techniques

Bead embroidery is all about using some basic embroidery stitches with beads added onto the thread for extra texture and color. Once you have mastered some simple techniques, you will be able to create your own items from scratch or embellish store-bought items, such as purses, cushions, or clothes.

Starting and ending thread

When you start a thread in bead embroidery, you need to think about whether the back of the work is going to show. There are two main methods for starting and ending a thread, and what you use depends on the look you are trying to achieve.

Starting and ending with a knot

It is perfectly all right to use knots in your work, especially if you are going to bead over the top, because the texture of the beads will usually hide the bump of the knot.

1 | To join a new thread to your fabric or beading surface, simply tie a knot at the end of the thread. Make sure the knot is larger than the width of the needle and, therefore, the hole you're going to make in the fabric. If the knot is too small, it may slip through the fabric as you bead, and if it is too large, it may be bulky and show through to the front.

2 | To finish a thread, bring the needle and thread to the back of the work and tie a knot, making sure you get it as close as you can to the fabric. If you need to, place a large, blunt needle or awl into the knot, as shown under the Knotting technique (see page 39), to help you guide the knot to the position you want.

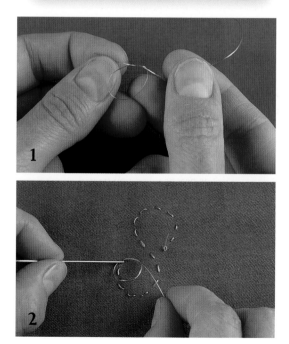

Bead Embroidery Techniques

Using hidden starts and ends

This method hides the start and end of a thread. You may want to use this technique if the back of the work is more likely to show.

Starting a thread

1 | Starting at the front of the fabric and working on a line you are going to bead, take the needle and thread through to the back, about ¼ in. (½ cm) to the right of where you will start beading. Do this in a place you will bead over so that the thread end will not show. Pull the thread through so that only a small length of it shows at the front.

2 | Bring the needle and thread up through the fabric, about ¼ in. (½ cm) over to the left from where you entered the fabric, again making sure you do this in an area that will be covered with the beadwork.

3 | Take the needle and thread back down into the fabric, just to the right of where you originally entered the fabric. Then bring the needle and thread up through the fabric at the point where you want to start beading.

4 | As you bead, you will cover the area where you added the thread and secure the thread even more.

Ending a thread

When you come to end the thread, it is important to keep the finish as neat as when you started.

Take the needle down into the fabric. If you have finished beading, make sure you end the thread so that it sits under the previous beading. However, if you still have beading to do, you can finish the thread off in a section that will later be covered with beads. Bring the needle and thread up through the fabric, and repeat how you started the thread, looping through the fabric until the thread is secured; then trim.

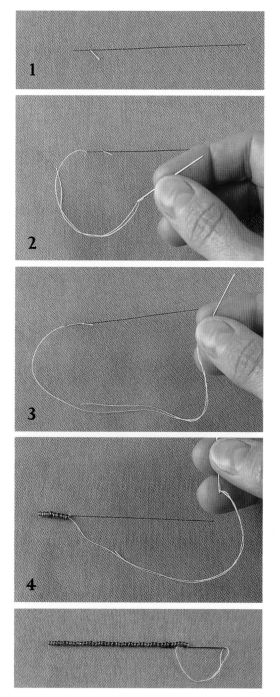

Bead Embroidery Techniques

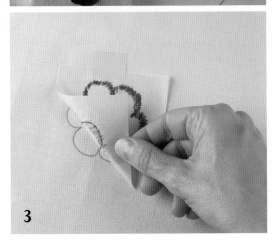

Transferring designs

When you are doing any bead embroidery, you may want to transfer your design onto the fabric. There are two ways of doing this, but remember, you can always draw your design freehand in pencil directly onto the fabric to add your own touch to the design.

Before you decide which technique to use, experiment on scraps of fabric first, to make sure that any marks you make can be washed off or easily removed. For some designs, such as the flowers on the Flower-embroidered napkins project (see pages 142–145), you don't need to transfer the whole design but simply indicate where the stitches are to start and finish.

Transferring with tracing paper

This method works best on light-colored fabrics, where the pencil lines show clearly.

1 | Lay a piece of tracing paper or baking parchment over the design. If it is a complicated design, tape it down with masking tape to make sure the paper doesn't move while you are copying it. Using a pencil, copy the design onto the tracing paper. Make sure you keep the lines as neat and exact as possible because any mistakes will be magnified as you go along.

2 | When you have copied the design, take the tracing paper off the design, turn it over, and draw over the lines with a pencil, placing a piece of scrap paper under it so as not to damage the work surface.

3 | Turn the tracing paper over so the design comes out the right way, and lay it over the fabric. Tape or pin it in place. Using the pencil, rub over the pencil lines you traced in Step 1. The pencil lines made in Step 2 will now be transferred onto the fabric.

Bead Embroidery Techniques

Transferring with carbon paper

Dressmaker's carbon paper can be used to transfer designs quickly onto the fabric. Photocopy the design so it is easier to use. This is especially recommended if your chosen design has been taken from a book.

1 | Place the carbon paper over the fabric, ink side down, and cover it with the design facing up. Secure the layers with masking tape. Do not use pins, because they will transfer carbon onto the fabric.

2 | Using a ballpoint pen, trace over the design, making sure you go over all the lines. Separate the layers and make sure the design has been transferred.

Using an embroidery hoop

An embroidery hoop is a useful tool for bead embroidery. It holds the work flat and makes it easier for you to bead.

As you bead, you may find you will need to readjust the hoop and fabric from time to time because it may lose its tension as you work.

1 | Lay the plain hoop down on a flat surface and place the fabric or item to bead over it.

2 | Lay the hoop with the tightening screws over the top and begin turning the screw. Make sure the fabric is flat and that it is neither pulled too tight nor lies too loose, because this will affect your work.

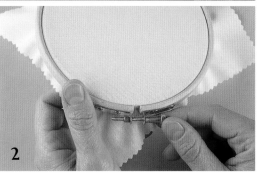

Bead Embroidery Techniques

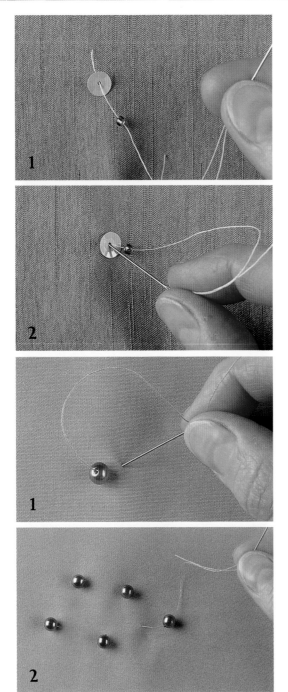

Sewing on sequins

Sequins, or spangles, can be used with beads to add decoration, color, and sparkle to your work. Sequins are small pieces of colored plastic or metal, usually round and sparkling. They have a hole in the center that is used to sew them down.

1 | Bring the needle and thread up through the fabric. Pick up 1 sequin and 1 bead. If the sequin has different sides, make sure that you go through it on the opposite side to the one you want to show.

2 | Skipping the bead, go down through the hole in the sequin again and then through the fabric to secure. Continue adding sequins until you have finished your design.

Adding single beads

When decorating an item in bead embroidery, it can be just as effective and decorative to sew on single beads as to cover your work densely with beads.

1 | Bring the needle and thread up through the fabric. Pick up 1 bead and go back into the fabric, entering the fabric at a distance that is about the same width as the bead.

2 | Continue adding single beads as close together or as wide apart as you like to finish your design.

Bead Embroidery Techniques

Backstitch

Backstitch is used in bead embroidery to outline items and draw pictures. In the instructions below, you pick up 4 beads each time, but sometimes you may need to pick up more. Look at the line you're beading for guidance.

1 | Bring the needle and thread up through the fabric on which you are beading. Pick up 4 beads and take the needle and thread down into the fabric. Make sure you enter the fabric at a distance that is about the same length as the bead so the beads lie flat.

2 | If you go in too close to where you exited, the beads will bunch up and not lie flat.

3 | Conversely, if you enter too far away from where you exited, the beads will spread apart and you will see lots of thread.

4 | Bring the needle and thread back up through the fabric, halfway along the line of beads. Make sure you come up directly below the beads so the thread is hidden.

5 | Go back through the last 2 beads in the line. Pick up 4 more beads and go into the fabric, following the instructions above, at the correct place.

6 | Repeating Step 4, come up through the fabric so you exit halfway along the line of 4 new beads.

7 | Repeat, adding beads and backstitching until you have covered the line in your design.

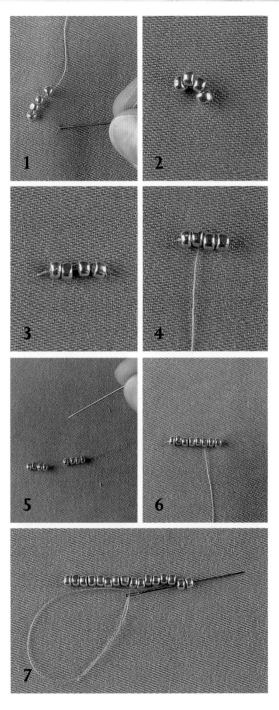

Bead Embroidery Techniques

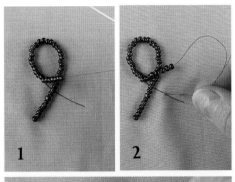

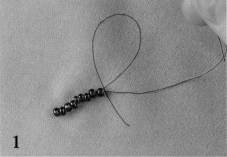

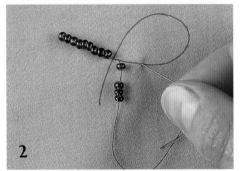

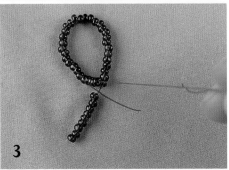

Backstitch: beading one line over another

When beading with backstitch, you may find that the line you are beading crosses over itself at some point. There are two ways in which you can deal with this. The first technique creates a 3D effect, with one line physically crossing the other. The second produces a flat look, with the beads fitting together.

One line over another

1 | Bead the line, using regular backstitch, until you reach the point where the lines cross. Pick up enough beads to cross over the line and go a little beyond; then take the needle and thread into the fabric.

2 | Bring the needle and thread up through the fabric to backstitch through the beads, making sure you do this after the crossover. Continue beading, as normal.

Gap in the line

1 | Bead the line using regular backstitch until you reach the point where the lines cross. When beading over the section where the lines cross, pick up the beads and take the needle and thread into the work, making sure you go in the length of 1 bead more than you need to.

2 | Continue beading until you reach the point where the lines cross, making sure you do not close up the gap with the next stitch.

3 | Pick up the beads, as before, and lay them over the line, making them lie in the space created in Step 2. Then continue beading.

Bead Embroidery Techniques

Chain stitch

Chain stitch is used to create motifs and is perfect for petal and leaf shapes. You can vary the way the stitch looks by varying how many beads you use in each step and where you make the second stitch.

1 | Bring the needle and thread up through the fabric and pick up 16 beads. Take the needle and thread back down into the fabric. Make sure you enter the fabric just to the right or left of where you exited.

2 | Lay down the beads so they lie flat. This will help in placing the next stitch. Bring the needle and thread up through the center of the bead loop. How close you bring the needle to the loop is your choice. Experiment until you achieve the look you like.

3 | Pick up approximately 5 to 6 beads. Lay them down over the beaded loop and check that you have picked up the right amount to fit comfortably over the loop and reach the fabric.

4 | Take the needle and thread down into the fabric to create the stitch that holds the loop in place. Repeat the motifs until you have created your design or pattern.

Wirework Techniques

By using a few simple tools, wire, and beads, you can create your own designer silver or gold jewelry. Just a handful of techniques will give you the ability to create pieces for all occasions.

Wirework Techniques

Cutting wire

When cutting wire, always keep safety in mind. Remember to wear safety glasses and to keep your fingers well away from sharp blades.

1 | Keep your fingers away from the blades of the wire cutters, and point the end you are cutting downward so no wire can fly up toward you or get into your eyes. Keep hold of the end you are cutting off so it doesn't fly away.

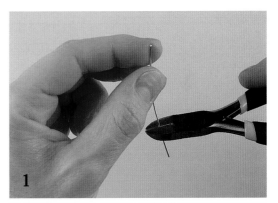

1

2 | If cutting memory wire, make sure you use memory wire cutters. You may find this wire impossible to cut with regular wire cutters, and the memory wire may permanently damage the cutters.

2

Turned loops

Turned loops are simple to make using round-nose pliers. Because these pliers come in various sizes, the loop size will differ and, therefore, how much wire you require will vary. Always start with a longer length of wire than you need and trim it as you go.

1 | Cut a length of wire at least the length of the bead, plus 1½ in. (4 cm). Look at the pliers and see where they are roughly the same size as you would like the loop to be. This is where you need to hold the wire on the pliers. When turning all the other loops in the piece, make sure you use the same section of the pliers. To help you with this, you can mark the pliers with a permanent marker or put a small piece of masking tape on the jaws.

2 | Holding the very end of the wire with the pliers, begin to turn the pliers to form a loop. Stop when the wire touches itself.

3 | With the pliers still in the loop, adjust the loop so that it sits centrally below the length of wire. Measure how much wire is left, excluding the loop. The difference between this and the original length is how much wire you will need to form a loop.

4 | Thread the bead onto the wire and, using your thumb, bend the wire end without a loop so it sits at a right angle to the bead. Cut this length of wire just slightly longer than the amount you calculated you would need to form the loop.

5 | Hold the end of the wire with the round-nose pliers in the same place on the jaws as when you turned the previous loop, and begin to turn a loop. Stop when you are satisfied with the loop. You can adjust it slightly with the pliers until you are happy with it.

Wirework Techniques

Wrapped loops

Wrapped loops are more secure than turned loops and add a decorative finish to beads and your work. They are slightly more complicated, but practicing them will help you achieve a neat finish.

Note: Unlike turned loops, wrapped loops cannot be opened once they are made. You will either need to join or attach them to other things afterward, using jump rings, or as you are making the loop in Step 3. Join this onto a previous loop and then start wrapping.

1 | Thread the bead onto a head pin. Rest the needle-nose pliers on the bead and, using your thumb, bend the wire so it sits at a right angle.

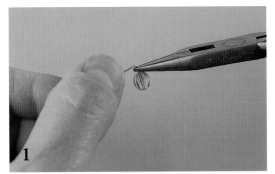

2 | Hold the end of the wire with your fingers or the needle-nose pliers and bend it around the round-nose pliers to form a loop. Stop when the wire crosses itself and points again at a right angle from the bead.

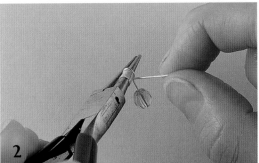

3 | Put the loop you have just made onto the round-nose pliers and, holding the cut end of the wire, begin wrapping it around the wire coming from the bead. Continue wrapping until you reach the bead.

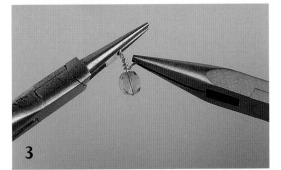

4 | Cut the wire as close to the work as possible; then press in the end using the pliers (crimping or needle-nose are best) for a neat finish. If you are not putting the bead onto a head pin but want to create a wrapped loop at each end, make the first wrapped loop; then thread the bead on and continue from Step 1 until you have a loop at each end.

Wirework Techniques

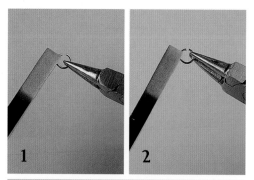

Opening and closing rings

All rings, such as jump rings and any on findings, must be opened sideways so as not to damage the ring or distort its round shape. You can use flat-, round-, or needle-nose pliers to hold, open, or close the rings. Simply use whatever you have or feel most comfortable with.

1 | Hold the ring with flat- or round-nose pliers on either side of the opening. Pull one pair of pliers toward you while moving the other away from you. Do this until you have an opening big enough to slip on what you want.

2 | Close the ring in the same way by pushing the ends back together again.

3 | If the ring is on a finding, you may hold it with only one pair of pliers. Hold the finding in your hand instead of using a second pair of pliers.

Making a homemade chain

Store-bought chains are perfect for embellishing with charms and beads. However, there are times when you will want a chain that is a specific length or need to extend a piece of jewelry by adding an extender chain. Here are instructions for making a custom-made chain.

1 | Using the technique described for opening and closing jump rings (see above), close 1 jump ring until the gap is as small as you can make it.

2 | Open another jump ring and link it through the closed ring. Close this second ring as neatly as you can. Continue closing rings and adding new ones until the chain is the length you need.

3 | You can make a double chain by adding extra rings into each space to create a double-looped chain that looks thicker and will be stronger.

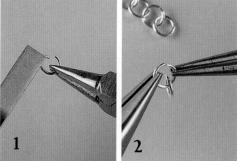

General Beading

Bead-Fringed Throw

This bold fringed throw uses natural and brown wooden beads in two different shapes strung on cord. You can use bold wooden beads for a natural look or brightly colored ones to jazz up the throw—the choice is yours.

Skill level: BEGINNER
Time: 5 hours

Bead-Fringed Throw

Materials

- Throw, made from fleece or other nonfray material
- Wooden beads in 2 different shapes and colors
- Brown leather cord that will fit through the holes in the beads

(See Step 1 for how to work out bead and cord quantities.)

Tools

- Tape measure
- Large blunt needle or awl
- Scissors

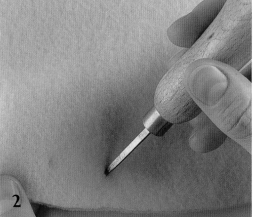

1 | To work out how much leather cord and how many beads you will need, measure around the 4 edges of the throw. For every 2 in. (5 cm) you will need:

- 4 × 8-mm round light wood beads
- 2 × 6 × 12-mm oval dark wood beads
- 10 in. (25 cm) brown leather cord

So for a throw measuring 170 in. (431 cm) all around, you will need approximately 340 round light wood beads, 170 oval dark wood beads, and 71 ft. (21.5 m) leather cord.

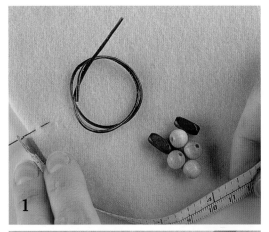

2 | Use the blunt needle or awl to make a hole every 1 in. (2.5 cm) around the edges of the throw. Make these holes approximately ⅝ in. (1.5 cm) in from the edges and be sure that you make an even number of holes on each side of the throw.

3 | Cut a 10-in. (25-cm) length of leather cord. This will give you the length you need plus a little more for the knots. Tie an overhand knot at one end, using the blunt needle or awl to guide it to the end, if necessary.

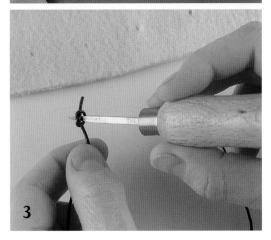

Bead-Fringed Throw

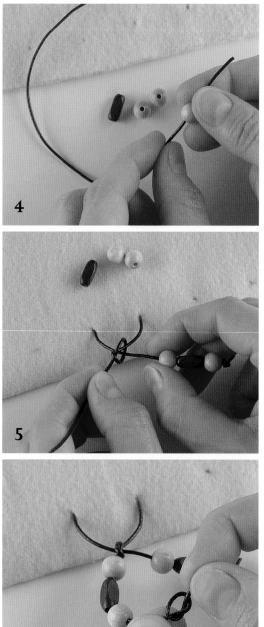

4 | Thread 1 round light wood bead onto the cord, then 1 oval dark wood bead and 1 round light wood bead again.

5 | Take the unknotted end of the cord through a hole in the throw, from front to back, leaving 2½ in. (6 cm) of the beaded cord hanging down. Bring the end of the cord through the next hole, from back to front. Tie the end of the cord around the beaded length, roughly 1½ in. (4 cm) from the knotted end.

6 | Thread on 1 round light wood bead, 1 oval dark wood bead, then 1 round light wood bead again. Tie a knot at the end of the cord; make sure that this side of the cord is the same length as the other. Trim the cord as necessary to complete. Repeat Steps 3 to 6 until you have completed the throw.

Bead-Fringed Throw

Beaded Tassel Cover

This project makes a store-bought tassel come alive with very simple beading. The tubular cover is square-stitched and is finished off with a beautiful fringed edge. If you can't find a tassel the same size as the one used here, you can easily modify the instructions to work with tassels of any size.

Skill level: ADVANCED
Time: 15 hours

Beaded Tassel Cover

Materials

* Reel of gold beading thread
* 1 store-bought tassel in shades of gold (approximately 5 in. / 12 cm in length)
* 504 size 11 rainbow luster rocaille beads in gold
* 154 size 11 rainbow luster rocaille beads in bronze
* 126 size 11 metallic luster seed beads
* 7 × 10-mm metallic luster twisted bugles
* 7 × 3-mm rainbow luster cubes in gold
* 7 × 3-mm metallic luster cubes in bronze
* 7 × 7-mm crystal rounds with gold lining

Tools

* #10 beading needle
* Scissors

1 | Using the gold beading thread, make a flat piece of square stitch following the design here. Be sure to use the diagram the right way around so that when the piece is sewn into a tube, the holes of the beads are at the top and bottom, since the fringe is sewn on through them. (See the Techniques section on page 32 for square-stitch instructions.)

2 | Holding the piece of square stitch to the tassel, sew up the sides using the same stitch but going through the beginning and end rows. You should now have a tube of beadwork around the neck of the tassel.

1

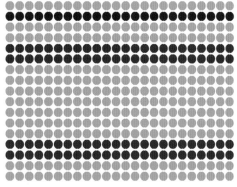

* size 11 rainbow luster rocaille in gold
* size 11 rainbow luster rocaille in bronze
* size 11 metallic luster seed bead

2

Beaded Tassel Cover

3 | Thread the beading thread into the needle and sew the end into the beads. Bring the needle out of a bead at the top of the beaded tube. You are now going to make a picot edge to neaten the top edge of the beadwork. Pick up 3 metallic luster seed beads and take the needle down into the next bead along. Go down 2 beads into the square stitch and bring the needle out. Push the needle back into the next bead on the right and up out of the top edge. Thread on 3 beads and continue in the same way until you have done this all around the top edge. This is known as a picot edge. Once you have completed the picot edge, thread the needle all the way down to the bottom edge of the beaded tube, ready to begin the fringe.

4 | Use the diagram on the opposite page to thread the beads on for the fringing. The beads should be threaded on following this sequence:

    2 metallic luster

    6 rainbow luster gold

    2 metallic luster

    2 rainbow luster gold

    1 rainbow luster gold cube

    2 rainbow luster gold

    1 twisted bugle

    2 rainbow luster gold

    1 bronze cube

    2 rainbow luster gold

    6 rainbow luster bronze

    2 rainbow luster gold

    1 crystal with gold lining

    1 rainbow luster gold

Now put the needle back up through the beads you have added and come out at the rainbow luster gold cube. Pull tight so that the beads cover all the thread running through them. Add on 2 rainbow luster gold, 2 metallic luster, 6 rainbow luster gold, and 2 metallic luster. Insert the needle in 3 beads along and 4 beads

Beaded Tassel Cover

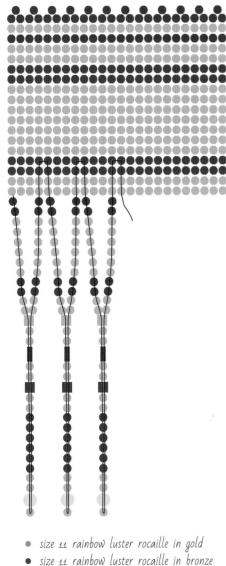

- size 11 rainbow luster rocaille in gold
- size 11 rainbow luster rocaille in bronze
- size 11 metallic luster seed bead
- 10-mm metallic luster twisted bugles
- 3-mm metallic luster cubes in bronze
- 3-mm rainbow luster cubes in gold
- 7-mm crystal rounds with gold lining

into the square-stitched collar and pull the thread tight. You have now completed the first fringe. Repeat this all the way around.

5 | When you have completed the last fringe, sew the thread into the square-stitch tube (see the Techniques section on page 32) and make sure all threads are secured and sewn in.

Note: If you are using a different-sized tassel, follow the instructions below so that the cover fits.

Make a sample piece of square stitch to see how long and wide you need to make it so that it fits around the neck of your tassel. Count the number of rows and make sure that it is divisible by 4. Follow the instructions for the main tassel, but add or decrease the fringing where necessary. If it is impossible to make the piece divisible by 4, then you will need to change the spacing of the fringing to work evenly around the number you decide on. It must, however, be an even number for the picot edging to work.

Square-Stitch Belt

Looking for a sturdy technique to stand the test of time? Stitch this attractive square-stitch belt with ribbon fastenings that will be the envy of all your friends.

Skill level: INTERMEDIATE
Time: 50 hours

Square-Stitch Belt

Materials
- Reel of pink Nymo "D" thread
- 60–70 g size 10 or 11 silver-lined pink seed beads
- 40–50 g size 10 or 11 opaque baby pink seed beads
- 36 in. (90 cm) pink ribbon

Tools
- #12 beading needle
- Scissors

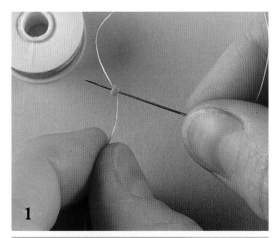

1 | Cut a piece of thread that you are comfortable working with and tie on a stop bead, leaving a 10-in. (25-cm) tail. This length of thread will be used later to make loops onto which the ribbon will be fastened.

2 | String 17 silver-lined pink seed beads—this will be the main color ("MC")—onto the thread to make Row 1.

3 | For Row 2, square-stitch (see the Techniques section on page 32) on 8 MC beads, 1 opaque baby pink seed bead—this will be the accent color ("AC")—and then 8 MC beads again.

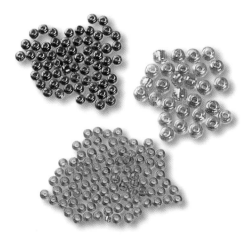

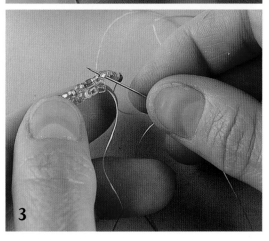

Square-Stitch Belt

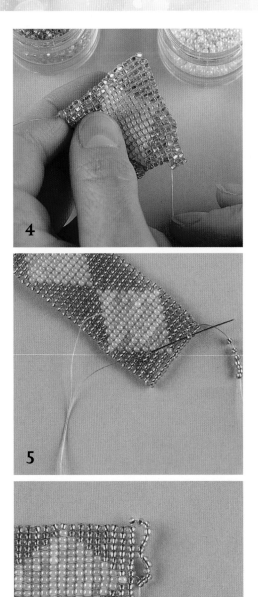

4 | Carry on square stitching to complete the following rows:

Row 3 = 7 MC, 3 AC, 7 MC
Row 4 = 6 MC, 5 AC, 6 MC
Row 5 = 5 MC, 7 AC, 5 MC
Row 6 = 4 MC, 9 AC, 4 MC
Row 7 = 3 MC, 11 AC, 3 MC
Row 8 = 2 MC, 13 AC, 2 MC
Row 9 = 1 MC, 15 AC, 1 MC
Row 10 = 2 MC, 13 AC, 2 MC
Row 11 = 3 MC, 11 AC, 3 MC
Row 12 = 4 MC, 9 AC, 4 MC
Row 13 = 5 MC, 7 AC, 5 MC
Row 14 = 6 MC, 5 AC, 6 MC
Row 15 = 7 MC, 3 AC, 7 MC
Row 16 = 8 MC, 1 AC, 8 MC

The above rows make a complete diamond. Keep repeating Rows 1 to 16 until the belt fits around your waist.

5 | There are 4 loops at either end of the belt through which the ribbon will be threaded.

- Loop 1: Come out of the last row of beads and string 6 MC beads. Square-stitch the last bead just strung onto the fourth bead in the last square-stitched row. String another MC bead and square-stitch this onto the next bead on the last row of the belt.

6 |

- Loop 2: String on another 6 MC beads and square-stitch the sixth bead to the ninth bead on the belt.
- Loop 3: String on another 6 MC beads, and again square-stitch the last bead to the thirteenth bead on the belt; then stitch another bead to the fourteenth bead.
- Loop 4: String on the last set of 6 MC beads and stitch in the last bead on the row from the outside edge. Backstitch through some previous beads, tying between beads to secure the thread.

Square-Stitch Belt

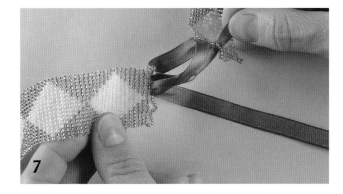

7 | Repeat Steps 5 and 6 to make the loops on the other side of the belt; then crisscross the ribbon through the loops as you would on your sneakers. The belt is then slipped over your head.

Netted Hoop Earrings

These bead-embellished hoop earrings are eye-catching and fun to wear. They are quick to make and can be adapted to suit many different outfits. Choose colors that are as wild or subtle as you like! The quantities stated below may vary, depending on the size of the hoop earrings.

Skill level: INTERMEDIATE
Time: 2 hours

Netted Hoop Earrings

Materials

- 1 pair silver hoop earrings
- 5 g size 11 seed beads in a range of greens
- Approximately 18 green 30 × 10-mm dagger beads (1 bead per loop for each earring)
- Reel of green beading thread

Tools

- Scissors
- #12 beading needle

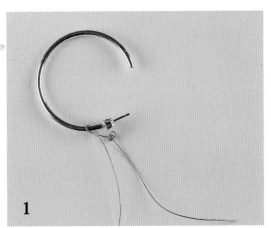

1 | Cut a 3-ft. (90-cm) length of beading thread and add a stop bead at least 3 in. (7.5 cm) from one end. Thread the needle and pick up 1 seed bead. Then, starting at either end of the hoop, loop over the hoop and bring the needle and thread back down the bead. Make sure that the bead sits along the outside rim of the hoop earring.

1

2 | Continue adding single seed beads in this manner, alternating the colors as you go until you have covered the outer rim of the hoop or beaded as much as you would like. Make sure you have added a number of beads that is a multiple of 4 plus 1 (i.e., 13, 17, 21, 25, 29, 33, 37, 41, etc.).

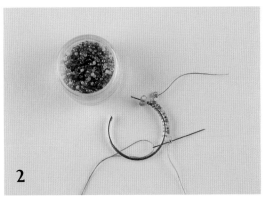

2

Netted Hoop Earrings

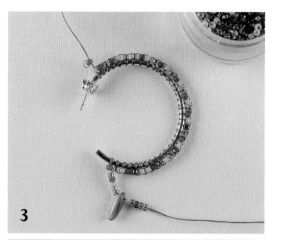

Crafter's Tip

Think about what size earrings will suit you, and adjust the number of beads in each loop accordingly. You could make the loops shorter for a more delicate earring or longer for a bolder earring; you could also add extra rows. See the "Fringed Scarf" project on pages 82–85 for ideas.

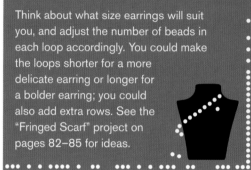

3 | Now pick up 5 seed beads, 1 dagger or drop bead, and 5 seed beads.

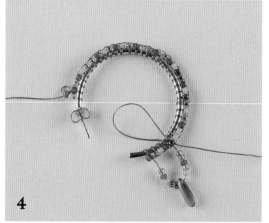

4 | Skipping the bead on the hoop that you are currently exiting, and the next three along, take the needle and thread up through the next bead, over the hoop, and down that bead again. Then go through the last bead you picked up in Step 3, which is the next bead along.

5 | This time pick up 4 seed beads, 1 dagger or drop bead, and 5 seed beads.

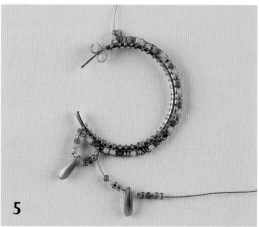

Netted Hoop Earrings

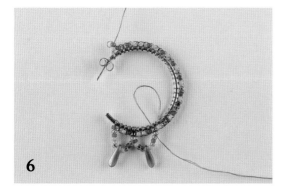

6

6 | Skipping the bead you are currently exiting, and the next three along the hoop, take the needle and thread through the next bead, over the hoop, and back down that bead again and the last one you added.

7

7 | Repeat Steps 5 and 6 until you have worked your way back to the start. Weave the thread through the work to secure and finish. Then remove the stop bead and weave this thread end in too, to secure.

Peyote-Stitch Pendant

Make this pretty floral-colored pendant in peyote stitch. You can hang it on a length of cord to wear it casually or on some pretty ribbon for an evening party look.

Skill level: INTERMEDIATE
Time: 4 hours

Peyote-Stitch Pendant

Materials

- Reel of purple Nymo "D" thread
- 1 g size 10 or 11 purple seed beads
- 1 g size 10 or 11 yellow seed beads
- 1 g size 10 or 11 blue seed beads
- 1 g size 10 or 11 pink seed beads
- 1 g size 10 or 11 green seed beads
- 26 in. (65 cm) satin cream cord
- 2 cord endings
- 2 jump rings
- 1 clasp

Tools

- #12 beading needle
- Scissors
- Flat-nose pliers
- Round-nose pliers

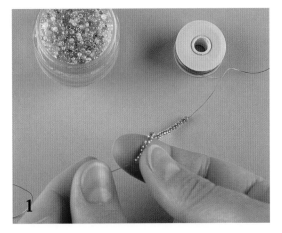

1 | Cut a 36-in. (90-cm) length of thread—or a length of thread you are comfortable working with—and string on a stop bead, leaving a 20-in. (50-cm) tail. String on 38 purple beads. (Purple will be the main color.) This will make up the first 2 rows of the pendant.

2 | Following the peyote-stitch instructions given in the Techniques section on pages 29–30 and using the diagram to the right, finish beading the pendant. Following the pattern, bead in the colors in the following sequence: purple, yellow, blue, pink, green, and then purple again. You will need 37 rows to complete the pendant. Once you have finished the last row, backstitch through some previous rows, tying a knot between some of the beads to secure the thread.

Peyote-Stitch Pendant

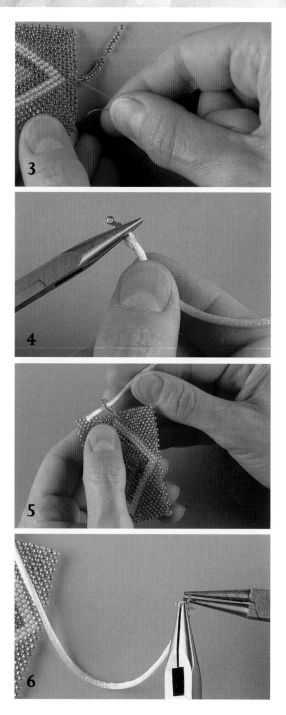

3 | To create the loop at the top of the pendant for the cord to go through, remove the stop bead from Step 1 and thread the tail that you left in Step 1 onto the needle. Work the thread through the beads of your pendant until the thread exits the center bead (which should be the tenth bead in from either end) at the top of the pendant, and string on 15 seed beads in the main color. Go back through the tenth bead you just exited on the pendant and work the thread down and back up the center 2 rows of the pendant; then go through the 15 beads just strung. Do this a couple of times to reinforce the loop.

4 | Measure and cut the cord on which the pendant will hang to the required length. Attach a cord ending to one end as explained in the Techniques section on page 40.

5 | String on the pendant; then add the second cord ending to the other end of the cord.

6 | To add the clasp to the cord ending, open the jump ring using two pairs of pliers and pass the ring through the loops of your cord ending and clasp. Close the jump ring and repeat for the other side.

Loom Bracelet

This checkered-effect loom-work bracelet is easy to make and ideal for beginners. It takes little more than an afternoon to complete and is the perfect project for those who have not used a loom before.

Skill level: BEGINNER
Time: 5 hours

Loom Bracelet

Materials
- Reel of blue Nymo "B" thread
- 2 g delica beads in green
- 2 g delica beads in blue
- 2 silver calottes
- 1 silver clasp

Tools
- Loom
- #12 beading needle
- Glue or clear nail polish
- Scissors
- Flat-nose pliers

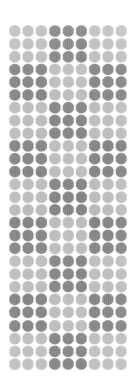

1 | Before you start, measure your wrist to determine the length of the bracelet. Subtract 1 in. (2.5 cm) from this measurement for the clasp. Set up the warp and weft threads as instructed in the Techniques section on page 33. You will need 10 warp threads.

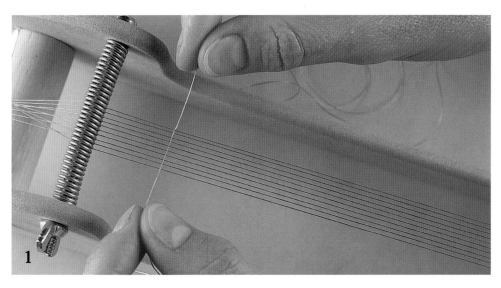

Loom Bracelet

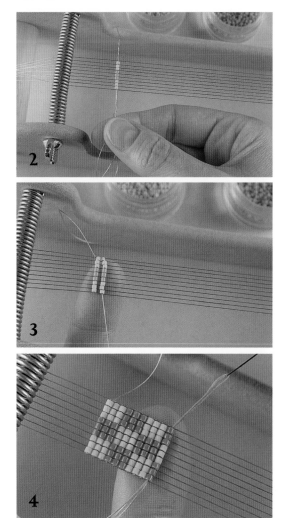

2 | Pick up 3 green beads, 3 blue beads, and 3 green beads. Secure the first row in place as explained in "Loom work—Adding rows," on page 33.

3 | Continue adding rows, using this technique, until you reach the length you require. The first 3 rows consist of 3 green beads, 3 blue beads, and 3 green beads. The following 3 rows (rows 4, 5, and 6) consist of 3 blue beads, 3 green beads, and 3 blue beads again.

4 | The rest of the bracelet now consists of alternating between the 2 colors. Every 3 rows you will need to change from one set of blue, green, blue to green, blue, green.

5 | Following the instructions given in the Techniques section on page 34, remove the bracelet from the loom, and finish off by attaching the calottes, allowing the warp threads to extend each side of the calottes.

6 | Finally, attach the hooks of the calottes to your clasp. Do this by threading the hook of the calotte through the loop of your clasp and squeezing it shut with the flat-nose pliers. Repeat this for the other side of the clasp and trim the threads.

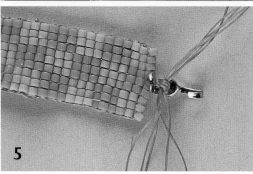

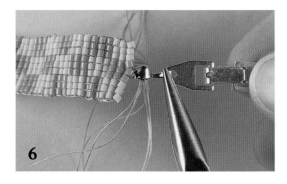

Loom Bracelet

Fringed Scarf

This embellished scarf uses bead netting and fringing to add a tactile, swaying fringe. You can use beads that coordinate or contrast with your scarf, or a mix of both. To make the fringe, start by adding a foundation of loops along the short sides of your scarf and add beaded netting to this foundation to create the fringe. Every time you step down to add a new layer of loops, you are starting a new row, and with each row the number of loops will decrease by one until you reach the last row with one loop in it. How many rows you need to add will depend on the width of your scarf.

Skill level: ADVANCED
Time: 4 hours

Fringed Scarf

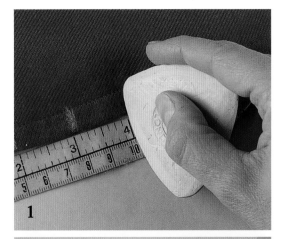

Materials
  * 1 scarf
  * Reel of beading or embroidery thread, to match the color of your scarf
  * Approximately 15 g size 11 seed beads, to match the color of your scarf

Tools
  * Measuring tape
  * Tailor's chalk
  * #12 beading needle
  * Scissors

1 | Using the measuring tape and the tailor's chalk, make 1-in. (2.5-cm) marks along both short sides of the scarf. You may have to alter the end marks a little so that they sit slightly more or less than 1 in. (2.5 cm) apart from the others. The end marks should be about ⅛ in. (2 mm) in from either edge.

2 | Thread the needle with a comfortable working length of thread and attach the thread to one of the end marks. Pick up 25 seed beads, then, missing the last bead added, take the needle and thread back through 24 beads. Make a small stitch through the lower edge of the scarf from the back to the front.

3 | Take the needle and thread back down through the last bead and pick up 23 seed beads. Take the needle and thread through the next mark along, again from back to front, and again come back down the last bead.

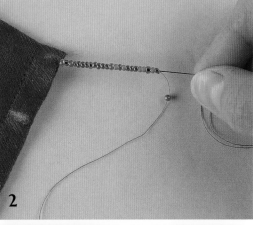

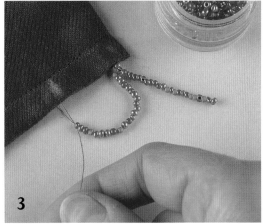

Fringed Scarf

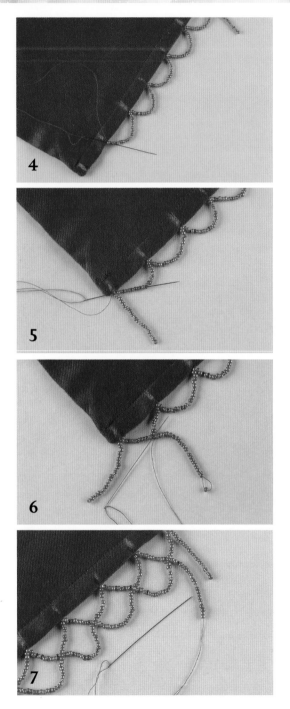

4 | Repeat picking up 23 seed beads and going through the next mark until you have gone through the last mark along the edge of the scarf.

5 | Making sure you have exited the last bead added, pick up 24 seed beads. Miss the last bead added and go back up all 24 beads. Take the needle and thread back through the scarf and down 12 seed beads in the last loop you beaded.

6 | Pick up 24 seed beads and, missing the last one, go back up through 23 beads and the bead you exited on the loop for a total of 24 beads. Make sure you go through this bead in the same direction you did previously so that you are in the right position to continue.

7 | Pick up 23 seed beads and go through the central bead on the next foundation loop. Repeat this until you have reached the last loop along, which was the first one you added. Now pick up 24 seed beads and, missing the last one, go back up through 23 beads and the bead you exited on the loop for a total of 24 beads. Make sure the needle is pointing in the right direction to carry on beading.

8 | Take the needle through 12 beads on the last loop you added in the last row. Pick up 24 beads and, missing the last one, go back up through 23 beads and the bead you just exited on the loop for a total of 24 beads. Make sure you go in the same direction so that the needle is facing the right direction to carry on the row.

9 | Pick up 23 beads and take the needle and thread through the central bead of the next loop along.

Fringed Scarf

10 | Continue linking the previously beaded loops with sections of 23 seed beads until you have reached the last one. Again, add a fringe of 24 seed beads and go back into the netting, making sure the needle is facing the right direction.

11 | Continue adding rows of loops and fringe until you have reached down to one central loop. Make sure you add a fringe of 24 seed beads on either side of the loop to match the previous rows; then add a fringe coming from the central bead in the loop. Weave your thread through your work to secure and finish. You will need to repeat all the steps for the other short side of the scarf.

12 | Once you have beaded all of the scarf, rub off the chalk marks and admire!

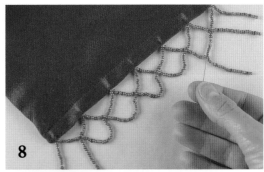

8

9

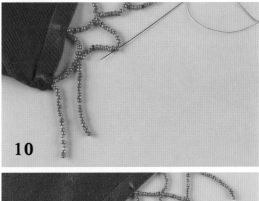

10

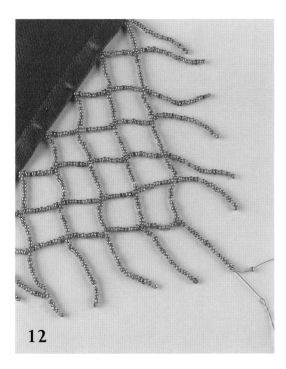

12

11

Bead-Fringed Lamp Shade

This fringed lamp shade is sure to add a touch of style to any room. Choose colors that either complement or contrast with your chosen lamp and shade, and have fun creating the fringe! This lamp shade uses size 9 seed beads, but if you have difficulty obtaining these, use size 10s or 11s instead.

Skill level: ADVANCED
Time: 25 hours

Bead-Fringed Lamp Shade

Materials

* 1 lamp shade with a 22-in. (56-cm) diameter at the base
* Reel of cream beading or embroidery thread
* 50 g size 9 cream seed beads (A beads)
* 15 g size 9 silver seed beads (B beads)
* 55 g size 9 black seed beads (C beads)
* 7 g size 9 gray seed beads (D beads)
* 15 g silver bugle beads (E beads)

Tools

* Measuring tape
* Two different-colored pencils
* #12 beading needle
* Scissors
* Paper

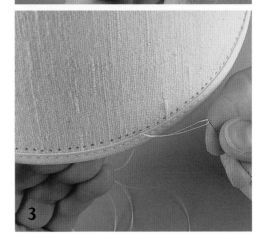

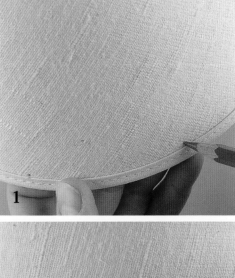

1 | Using the measuring tape, measure the circumference of the shade where the fringing will be. Divide this measurement by 4 and mark these quarter marks on the bottom edge with one of the colored pencils. Measure halfway between these marks, and again mark the bottom edge with the same pencil. You should now have 8 marks along the bottom edge. These marks indicate where the shortest and longest points of the fringe will fall.

2 | Using the measuring tape and the other colored pencil, make a mark every ⅛ in. (3 mm) between the marks you made in Step 1. There should be 23 marks between each of the marks made in Step 1.

3 | Secure a comfortable working length of thread—78 in. (2 m) is a good length—to the outside of the shade's frame, just above the metal edge. Make sure you exit at one of the first marked points you made.

Bead-Fringed Lamp Shade

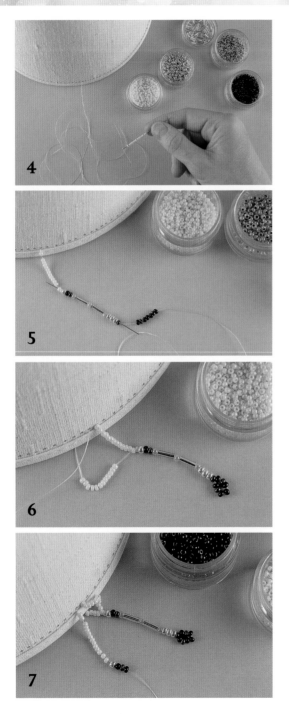

4 | Pick up the following combination of beads: 14 A beads—this is how many are shown in the photographs, but you may need to pick up a few more or less. You need an amount that will fit over the wire edge of the lamp shade and hang down slightly. Make a note of how many more or less you pick up than the instructions indicate; then make sure you add or subtract the same amount each time for the A beads. Continue adding the following sequence of beads:

> 1 B bead, *2 C beads*,
> 1 D bead, 1 E bead, 1 D bead,
> 1 E bead, 1 D bead, 3 B beads,
> 8 C beads.

5 | Missing the last 7 C beads, go back up 14 beads until you are 12 A beads from the top.

6 | Pick up 12 A beads and go through the frame from the outside to the inside, exiting at the next ⅛-in. (3-mm) mark along the edge of the frame.

7 | Pick up the same combination of beads as in Step 4, but when you reach the first set of C beads (marked with two *), pick up 3 C beads this time.

Bead-Fringed Lamp Shade

8 | Continue adding fringes, increasing the number of *C beads* you pick up each time one by one, until you reach the marked point that shows where the longest fringe in the sequence will be. Add the long fringe here, but from now on, decrease the number of *C beads* you pick up each time by one until you reach the mark indicating where the shortest fringe will fall.

9 | Continue adding fringes all the way around the lamp shade, remembering to increase and decrease the number of beads where necessary. As you bead, you will need to add new thread. This can be done by securing the thread you are working with inside the frame with a knot when it starts to get too short and adding a new thread in the same way as you started the first. When you reach the start and need to finish the thread, simply take the thread inside the shade and finish by knotting it securely. Thread the needle through a few beads to "loose" the thread end. Cut off the excess thread close to the fringe.

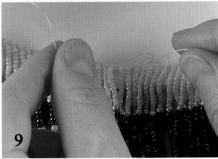

Stringing

Eyeglass Chain

A fashionable and convenient way to keep your glasses handy, this chain can be made with any leftover beads you have lying around. Alternatively, choose special beads that will give your chain a unique look and feel. Thanks to this chain, you will never have to go searching for your glasses again!

Skill level: BEGINNER
Time: 2 hours

Eyeglass Chain

Materials

- 32-in. (81-cm) length red glass chips
- 3 g size 10 or 11 red seed beads
- 3 g size 10 or 11 gold seed beads
- Flexible beading wire, 0.18
- 2 crimp beads
- 2 eyeglass holders

Tools

- Wire cutters
- Crimping pliers
- Flat-nose pliers

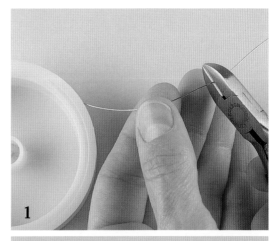

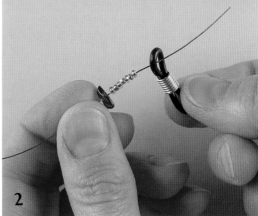

1 | Determine the finished length of your eyeglass holder and add 6 in. (15 cm) to the figure. Cut the beading wire to that length using the wire cutters. Here we have cut the wire to 32 in. (81 cm) plus the 6 in. (15 cm).

2 | On one end of the wire, string 1 chip, 3 seed beads (1 gold, 1 red, 1 gold), 1 crimp bead, 3 seed beads (1 gold, 1 red, 1 gold), and 1 eyeglass holder.

3 | Once you have threaded the eyeglass holder, go back through the beads you have just strung and tighten the wire by gently pulling it with the flat-nose pliers. Crimp the crimp bead using the crimping pliers.

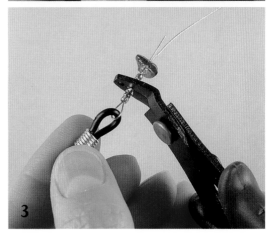

Eyeglass Chain

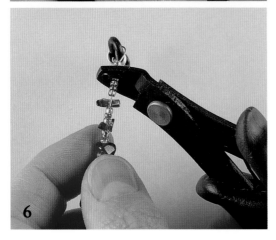

4 | Continue stringing the beads—1 chip, 3 seed beads (1 gold, 1 red, 1 gold)—from the other end of the wire until the strand is within ½ in. (1 cm) of the desired length. Finish off by stringing 3 seed beads.

5 | String a crimp bead, 3 more seed beads, and the other eyeglass holder. Go back through the beads you have just strung, plus a few more, and tighten the wire with the chain-nose pliers.

6 | Check that the fit is comfortable—you can add or remove beads as necessary. When you are happy with the length, crimp the crimp bead. Finish by trimming off the excess wire with the wire cutters.

Treasure Charm Necklace

This multistrand, leather-cord, knotted necklace is incredibly versatile and provides a great opportunity to use up all those single beads you have left over from other projects. Use charms, beads, and shells to decorate a long, continuous length of cord that you can wear in different ways. Wrap it around many times for a shorter necklace or fewer times if you prefer to wear it longer.

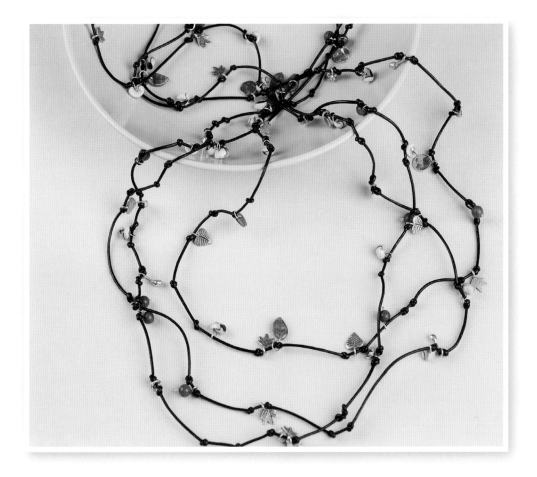

Skill level: INTERMEDIATE
Time: 5 hours

Treasure Charm Necklace

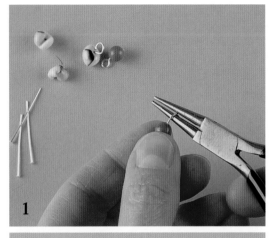

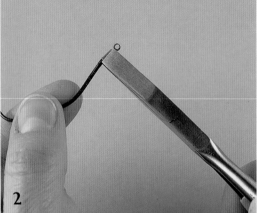

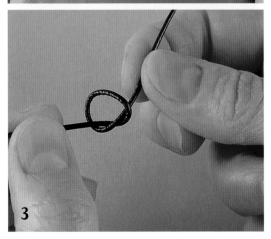

Materials
- 20 ft. (6 m) 2-mm brown leather cord—this length gives a finished necklace of around 12 ft. (3.7 m)
- Selection of about 80 silver charms, beads, and shells
- Silver head pins—you will need 1 head pin for each charm that cannot be threaded onto the cord.
- 2 silver cord endings
- 1 silver toggle clasp

Tools
- Scissors
- Round-nose pliers
- Flat-nose pliers
- Wire cutters

1 | Thread any charms, beads, or shells that do not have a big hole to feed the cord through onto head pins and make turned loops using the round-nose pliers (see the Techniques section on page 52). Cut the excess wire with the wire cutters.

2 | Place one end of the cord into a cord ending and, using the flat-nose pliers, crimp first one side of the cord ending and then the other to securely hold the cord in place.

3 | Tie an overhand knot approximately 2 in. (5 cm) from the cord ending.

Treasure Charm Necklace

4 | Thread on a charm, bead, or shell; then tie an overhand knot just beneath this treasure charm to stop it from sliding down the cord. Adding a knot on either side of the charm will stop it from sliding and gathering too close to another. This will mean that each charm will remain evenly spaced out over the length of the necklace. However, if you wish to keep some movement in the necklace, just tie one knot between each charm. Space the charms about 1½–2 in. (4–5 cm) apart.

5 | Continue tying knots and threading on charms, beads, and shells until you come within 2 ft. (60 cm) of the end of the cord. Try wrapping the necklace around in different lengths and amounts to check if it is the length you require. If the length embellished is not long enough, continue adding charms.

6 | When you are happy with the length, trim the cord; then add the other cord end and a clasp to finish.

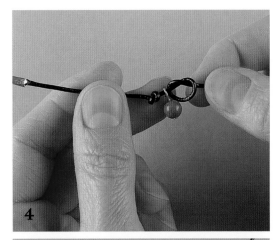

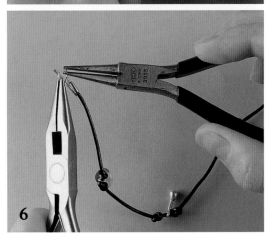

Knotted-Cord Necklace

Use knots to separate and frame individual beads in this bold necklace. Make sure the beads you choose fit comfortably onto the thickness of the cord.

Skill level: INTERMEDIATE
Time: 2 hours

Knotted-Cord Necklace

Materials

- 2-mm rust-colored cord (at least 3 times the finished length you require)
- 9 × 9-mm red beads
- 10 × 9-mm turquoise beads

Note: The beads must have holes large enough to fit the cord.

- 2 gold cord ends
- 1 gold toggle clasp
- 2 gold jump rings

Tools

- Scissors
- Glue or clear nail polish (optional)
- Large blunt needle or awl
- Flat-nose pliers

1 | Work out how long you want the necklace to be and cut a length of cord at least three times this length. If you need help threading the beads, apply glue or clear nail polish to the ends of the cord and cut into a point as described in the Techniques section on page 37.

2 | Tie an overhand knot in the cord, approximately 3 in. (7.5 cm) away from one of the glued ends.

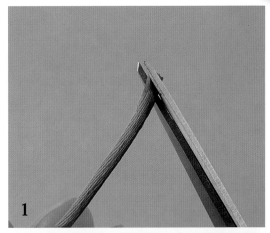

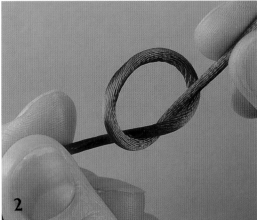

Knotted-Cord Necklace

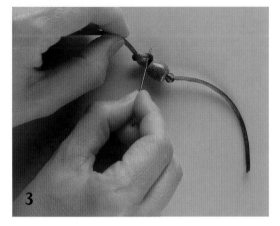

3

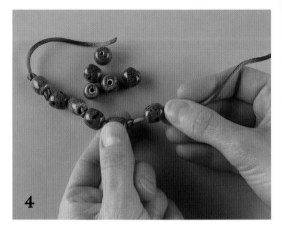

4

3 | Thread on 1 turquoise bead. Tie an overhand knot next to the bead to hold it in place. Use a blunt needle or awl to move the knot along if necessary (see the Techniques section on page 39).

4 | Repeat adding beads—alternating the colors—and knots to the necklace until it is the length you require.

5 | If you think your cord ends may fray, glue them as described in the Techniques section on page 37. Then, using the flat-nose pliers, attach a cord ending to each end and use a jump ring to attach each cord end to one end of the toggle clasp.

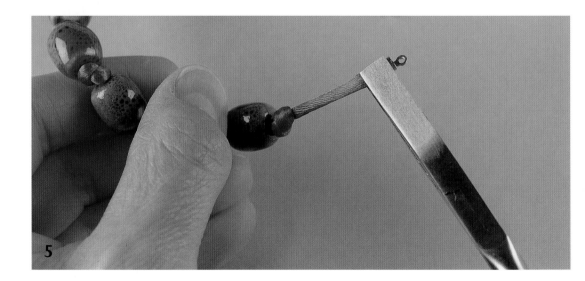

5

Wire-and-Bead Necklace

This simple and stylish necklace can be put together in a few minutes. Easy to make, it will be the envy of all your friends.

Skill level: BEGINNER
Time: 1 hour

Wire-and-Bead Necklace

Materials

- Silver flexible beading wire
- 8 crimp beads
- 3 silver jump rings
- 4 × 6-mm silver spacer beads
- 2 × 8-mm silver beads
- 1 green focal bead
- 1 silver lobster clasp

Tools

- Wire cutters
- Chain-nose pliers
- Crimping pliers

1 | Determine the length you would like your necklace to be and subtract 1 in. (2.5 cm) from this for the clasp. To determine the final length of the beading wire, add 6 in. (15 cm) to that figure. Cut a piece of wire to this length with the wire cutters.

2 | Thread 3 crimp beads and 1 jump ring on one end of the wire. Loop the wire through the jump ring and back through the 3 crimp beads. Tighten the wire and crimp the beads with the crimping pliers or chain-nose pliers. Cut off excess wire.

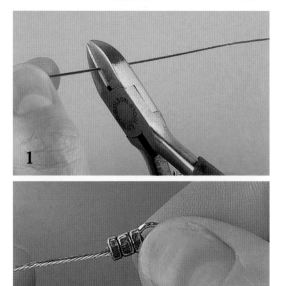

1

2

Wire-and-Bead Necklace

3 | From the other end of the wire, string 1 crimp bead, 1 spacer bead, 1 silver bead, 1 spacer again, the green focal bead, another spacer, the second silver bead, the last spacer bead, and then another crimp bead. These will be the focal point of your necklace.

4 | Thread on 3 crimp beads and 1 jump ring. Loop the wire through the jump ring and back through the 3 crimp beads. Tighten the wire and crimp the beads. Cut off excess wire.

5 | Adjust the focal beads until you are happy with where they sit in the center of your necklace. Then crimp the crimp beads on either side of the beads to hold them in place. Thread an open jump ring through the lobster clasp then through one of the jump rings at the end of the wire; then close the jump ring.

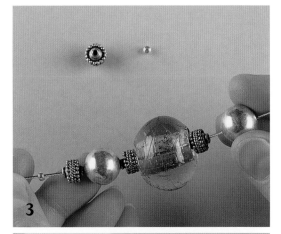

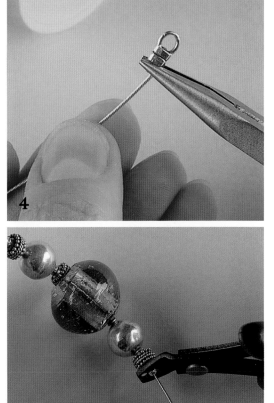

Pearl Necklace

This is a classic piece of jewelry that will suit anyone's wardrobe. Eternally popular, this simple single strand of pearls is bound to be one of your favorite pieces. Check that the pearls you'll use on the end have holes large enough for the beading wire to go through them twice. If the holes are too small, you can use a bead reamer to enlarge them.

Skill level: BEGINNER
Time: 2 hours

Pearl Necklace

Materials

* 16-in. (40.5-cm) strand of freshwater pearls
* Flexible beading wire
* 2 crimp beads
* 5 g size 11 silver seed beads
* 1 silver toggle clasp

Tools

* Wire cutters
* Crimping pliers or flat-nose pliers

1 | Decide on the length you would like the finished necklace to be. Taking into account the length of the clasp, cut a piece of flexible wire at least 3 in. (7.5 cm) longer than this length.

2 | Thread 1 crimp bead onto the beading wire and take the end of the wire through one end of the clasp. Then take the end of the wire back through the crimp bead. Make sure that the crimp sits at least ½ in. (1 cm) away from the end of the beading wire and that the clasp can move freely. Then crimp the crimp bead using either the crimping pliers or the flat-nose pliers.

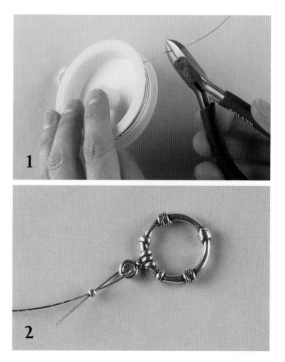

Pearl Necklace

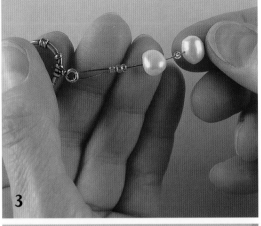

3 | Thread on 2 seed beads to cover the ends of the wire; then begin threading on a pattern of 1 pearl and 1 seed bead until you reach the required length. When you reach the end, thread on 2 seed beads to cover the wire ends.

4 | Add 1 crimp bead and go through the other half of the clasp and back through the crimp and at least one of the pearls. Check how the necklace lies by bending it, being careful not to drop all the pearls! You may find that for the pearls to rest comfortably around your neck and to sit next to one another correctly, there is a gap along the beading wire when it is laid flat. This is quite normal, and the gap disappears when the necklace is curved.

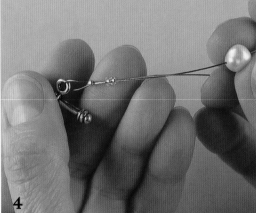

5 | Pull the end of the flexible beading wire tight so that the clasp is not free to move, and trim the wire as close as you can to the pearls. Gently pull on the clasp to loosen it so that the end of the wire disappears inside a bead. Crimp the crimp bead with the flat-nose pliers to finish.

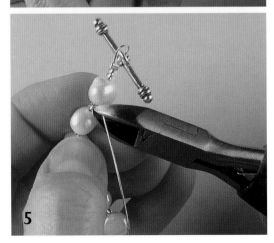

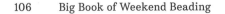

Pearl Necklace

Variation

Classic pearl necklace

You could also make this into a classic pearl necklace by using only pearl beads. Remember also that this basic technique applies to any beads. Get out your bead board and beads and play around designing pieces until you are happy with a combination, string them, and you'll soon build up a wardrobe of beautiful jewelry.

Elastic Bracelet

This elasticized bracelet is easy to make and lends itself to a number of possibilities: you can use pearls and crystals for an elegant evening look, or seed beads and letter beads for daywear. You can wear a single bracelet or several at a time. The choice is yours.

Skill level: BEGINNER
Time: 1 hour

Elastic Bracelet

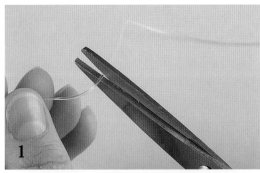

Materials

- 5 letter beads
- 10 × 4-mm round orange glass beads
- 25 × 3-mm burgundy cubes
- 14 in. (35 cm) clear elastic

Note: The thickness of the elastic will depend on the size of the holes of your beads.

Tools

- Scissors
- Glue

1 | Measure your wrist and add 5 in. (13 cm) to the figure; then cut the elastic to that size.

2 | String your chosen beads onto the elastic until you have strung the desired length. Check the fit, adding or removing beads as necessary.

3 | When you are happy with the size, tie the ends into a knot.

4 | Trim the elastic to ⅛ in. (3 mm) and apply a dot of glue to the knot. Gently pull the bracelet to hide the knot inside a bead.

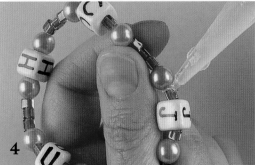

Ribbon Necklace

This necklace uses the contrast of ribbon and beads to great effect. The beads are held in place only by the ribbon running through them, and the hardest part is adding the clasp!

Skill level: INTERMEDIATE
Time: 2 hours

Ribbon Necklace

Materials

* 3 × 23-in. (58-cm) lengths green ½-in. (1-cm)-wide organza ribbon
* 3 × 23-in. (58-cm) lengths purple ½-in. (1-cm)-wide organza ribbon
* Wire ribbon needle (see the Techniques section on page 38)
* 45 beads with holes large enough to thread the ribbon through but not so big as to slide once threaded
* 2 × 3-in. (7.5-cm) lengths 18-gauge silver wire
* 2 × 2-mm silver bead cones
* 1 silver toggle clasp
* 1 × 6-in. (15-cm) length green ½-in. (1-cm)-wide organza ribbon
* 1 focal bead—larger than the other beads and in a toning color
* Glue (optional)

Tools

* Round-nose pliers
* Needle-nose pliers
* Wire cutters
* Scissors

1 | Thread one end of one of the 23-in. (58-cm) ribbons through the wire needle that you have made and randomly thread on the beads. There should be roughly 8 beads on each ribbon. Space them out evenly along the length. Repeat until all 6 lengths of ribbon are done.

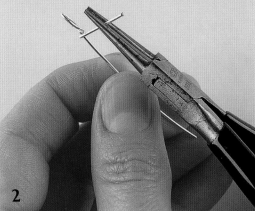

2 | Take one of the pieces of 3-in. (7.5-cm) silver wire and make a wrapped loop at one end (see the Techniques section on page 53), ensuring that the loop is big enough to thread through the ends of all 6 ribbons.

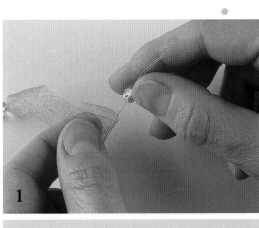

Ribbon Necklace

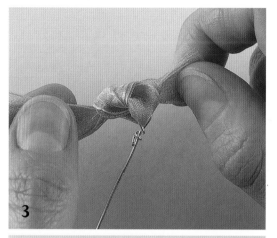

3 | Thread the end of the ribbons through the wrapped loop and double-knot onto the wire. Trim the excess with scissors. To make the knot more secure, you can dab a spot of glue on it.

4 | Thread a bead cone onto the other end of the wire and pull it down over the ribbon ends. Make a wrapped loop (see the Techniques section on page 53), adding one end of the toggle clasp before wrapping.

5 | Lay the necklace flat on the work counter and weave the ribbon (see diagram below). Repeat Steps 2 to 4 on the other end of the necklace.

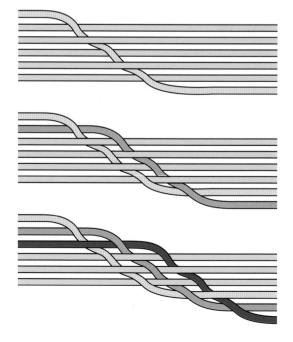

Ribbon Necklace

6 | Loop the 6-in. (15-cm) cut length of green ribbon over the center of the necklace and thread both ends through the focal bead of your choice. The hole should be small enough so that the bead stays in place by itself, but for extra security, knot into place. Then make a knot at the very end of both pieces of ribbon and trim the excess.

6

Variation

Cool and fresh ribbon necklace

This variation is made in exactly the same way but shows the versatility of the design by simply changing the colors of the ribbons and beads.

Illusion Necklace

This necklace is simple and easy to make and uses only one method: crimping beads onto flexible wire thread.

Skill level: BEGINNER
Time: 1 hour

Illusion Necklace

Materials

- 2 × 20-in. (51-cm) lengths 0.18-in. flexible beading wire
- 34 size 1 silver crimps
- 20 × 4-mm rose bicone crystals
- 11 × 6-mm pink freshwater pearls
- 2 calottes
- 2 × 4-mm silver jump rings
- 1 silver lobster clasp
- 1 silver extension chain

Tools

- Wire cutters
- Crimping pliers
- 2 flat-nose pliers

1 | Take one piece of flexible beading wire and thread on 1 crimp, 1 crystal, 1 pearl, 1 crystal, and 1 crimp. Slide all the beads into the middle of the wire and, using the crimping pliers, squash both crimps on either side of the beads to secure in place (see the Techniques section on page 37).

2 | Repeat Step 1 on either side of the beads, leaving a length of wire about 1½ in. (3.5 cm) between the next set of beads. Repeat until you have completed 7 sets.

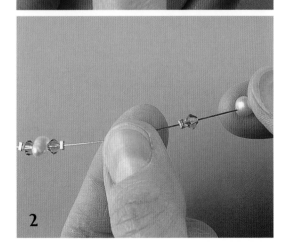

Illusion Necklace

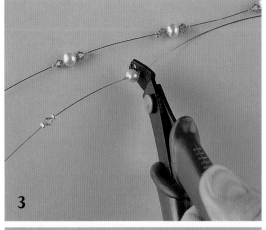

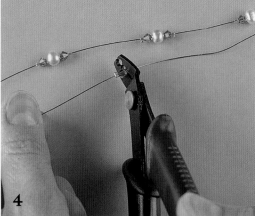

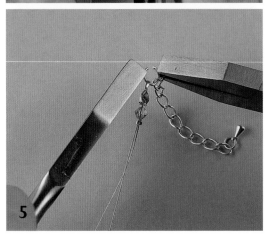

3 | Lay the beaded strand out flat and place the other piece of flexible beading wire next to it. On the empty wire, string 1 crimp, 1 crystal, and 1 crimp. Crimp into place so that the single crystal sits about halfway between two sets of 3 beads on the other wire.

4 | Repeat Step 3, alternating between crystals and pearls, until you have 8 sets of beads crimped into place. To finish each end, thread both pieces of wire through 1 crimp, 1 crystal, 1 open calotte, and 1 crimp. Leave 1 in. (2.5 cm) of wire on either side and crimp into place. Cut off the excess wire with wire cutters and close the calotte (see the Techniques section on page 41).

5 | Thread an open jump ring through the lobster-clasp fastening and the calotte, and then close the jump ring using the flat-nose pliers. Do the same at the other end, but with an extension chain instead of the clasp.

Illusion Necklace

Variation

Pearl-and-bead necklace

This variation necklace is made in exactly the same way but uses different-colored beads. This is a very versatile style that can be adapted to use a wide variety of beads. You can also try making the necklace with 1 strand or with 3 strands. Another option would be to use lots of beads in the center and gradually use fewer on either side. The possibilities are endless.

Bali-Bead Necklace

This elegant necklace, made with cat's-eyes and silver Bali beads, will look stunning on anyone. It can be worn as a traditional-length necklace or at the base of the neck as a choker. You could even wrap it around your wrist and wear it as a bracelet.

Skill level: INTERMEDIATE
Time: 3 hours

Bali-Bead Necklace

Materials

- Reel of Nymo "F" thread
- 1 silver lobster clasp
- 28 × 3-mm dark brown cat's-eyes beads
- 20 × 3-mm light brown cat's-eyes beads
- 9 × 6-mm silver Bali beads
- 14 × 6-mm dark brown cat's-eyes beads
- 10 × 6-mm light brown cat's-eyes beads
- 40 × 3-mm silver Bali spacers
- 2 × 12-mm silver Bali beads
- 6-in. (15-cm) silver chain, with loops big enough for the clasp to close through
- 1 × 6-mm silver jump ring

Tools

- Scissors
- Needle-nose pliers
- #12 beading needle

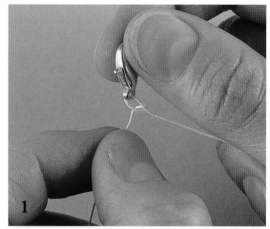

1

2

1 | Measure the base of your neck and cut the thread to three times this figure. String on the clasp to the center of the thread and tie a knot to hold the clasp in place.

2 | On each thread (and making sure you are stringing on beads of two different colors), string one 3-mm cat's-eyes bead, one 6-mm cat's-eyes bead, and one 3-mm cat's-eyes bead again. Once these are strung, pass both ends of the thread through a 6-mm Bali bead.

3 | Repeat the process again, this time adding Bali spacers in between each bead. So on each thread, string one 3-mm bead, 1 spacer, one 6-mm bead, 1 spacer, and one 3-mm bead again. As before, pass both threads through a 6-mm Bali bead.

3

Bali-Bead Necklace

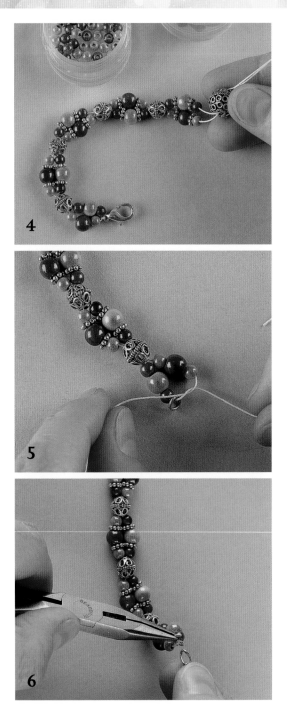

4 | Keep repeating this process until just before the halfway point. Now pass both ends of the thread through a 12-mm Bali bead. Repeat Step 3 twice, using only the 3-mm and 6-mm dark brown beads; then add another 12-mm Bali bead. Continue stringing the necklace, making sure that the last set of beads strung does not have any Bali spacers.

5 | String the jump ring on one of the threads and tightly knot both threads together.

6 | Wind both threads around the jump ring a couple of times; then pass each thread separately back through the strung beads, knotting in between. Cut off the excess thread. To make the necklace adjustable, you can add a length of chain to the end of the clasp. To do this, open a jump ring, thread on the chain, then go through the clasp and close the jump ring.

Bead Embroidery

Eyeglass Case

Small glass beads are formed into delicate flowers on this pretty eyeglass case. The hanging flowers are created with a clever beading technique, while the others are embroidered at random.

Skill level: INTERMEDIATE
Time: 2 hours

Eyeglass Case

Materials

* Pink fabric eyeglass case
* 5 g size 11 silver rocaille beads
* 2 g size 9 turquoise glass rocaille beads
* 14 size 9 green glass rocaille beads
* 12 size 9 silver rocaille beads
* 12 size 9 pale blue glass rocaille beads
* Reel of pink beading thread

Tools

* #10 beading needle
* 7 glass-headed dressmaking pins
* Pencil

1 | Sew a line of size 11 silver rocaille beads ⅜ in. (1 cm) below the upper edge of the eyeglass case using a backstitch.

2 | To make a flower stem, sew a line of size 11 silver rocaille beads along the center of the front of the eyeglass case for 1 in. (2.5 cm), starting at the upper beaded line, using a backstitch. Do not fasten off the thread.

3 | Thread on 6 size 11 silver rocaille beads, 4 turquoise glass rocaille beads, and 1 green glass rocaille bead.

4 | Insert the needle back through the first turquoise bead. Pull the thread to form half the flower.

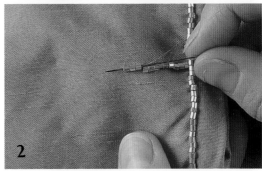

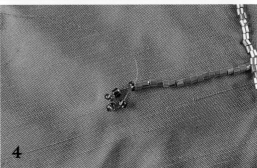

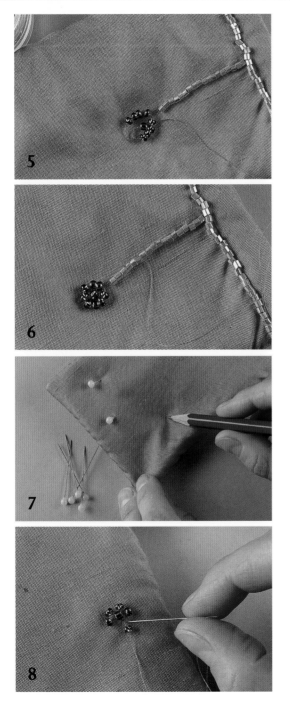

5 | Thread on 4 turquoise beads. Insert the needle back through the fourth, third, then second turquoise bead.

6 | Pull the thread so that the turquoise beads surround the green bead. Insert the needle back through the last 6 silver beads. Fasten the thread securely inside the case. Repeat to make 6 more stems of different lengths, with hanging flowers ⅝ in. (1.5 cm) apart.

7 | To mark the position of the random flowers, push 7 glass-headed pins into the front of the case at random. When you are happy with the arrangement, mark the flower positions with a pencil.

8 | Sew a green glass bead at one dot. Sew 6 turquoise glass beads around the green bead. Repeat at four of the other dots.

9 | Sew a green bead at one of the remaining dots. Sew 6 silver size 9 rocaille beads around the green bead. Sew 6 pale blue glass beads around the flower, keeping the spaces between them equidistant. Repeat at the last dot.

Eyeglass Case

Variation

Spring eyeglass case

This eyeglass case is worked in the same way as the main project. Copper-colored rocailles are used for the stems. The flower petals are metallic pink beads around a ⅛-in. (3-mm) purple pearl. The large, random flowers are outlined with silver and pink glass beads.

Embroidered Shawl

This bead-and-sequin—embellished shawl is sure to wow anyone who sees it! Using a simple circle motif, go as delicate or as wild as you like. Use a variety of stitches and looks to add as much interest as possible.

Skill level: ADVANCED
Time: 8 hours

Embroidered Shawl

Materials

- 1 cream-colored fringed shawl
- Reel of cream beading or embroidery thread
- 10–20 g seed beads (a mix of different colors and sizes)
- 8–10 g sequins in different sizes and in colors that match the beads

Tools

- Compass or circular items, for making circles
- Water-erasable pen
- Embroidery hoop (optional)
- #12 beading needle
- Scissors

1 | Place the shawl flat on your work surface. Place your choice of circular objects (e.g., teacup, glass, or can) over the shawl and lightly draw around them with a water-erasable pen. Alternatively, you could use a compass to make as many circles as you want to bead. The circles should be positioned haphazardly, toward the short ends of the scarf. They can be close together or far apart, separate or overlapping—the choice is yours! Before you draw the circles, check that they can be easily removed in case you change your design.

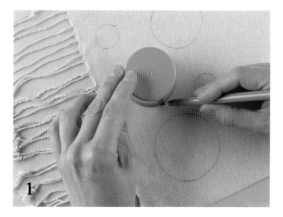

Embroidered Shawl

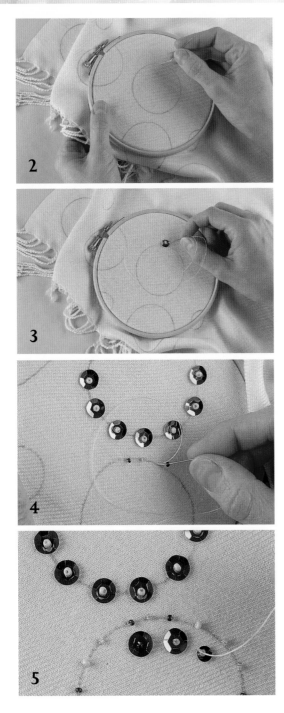

2 | Secure the section of shawl you are going to bead into the embroidery hoop, if you are using one. Then neatly attach a thread to the edge of one of the circles.

3 | Using the backstitch (see the Techniques section on page 47) or by adding single beads or sequins, bead the outline of one of the circles; then neatly finish off the thread. If you are adding single beads at a time, try to space them out evenly. When adding sequins, these can be secured in place with a seed bead. You can choose to use the same seed bead for each sequin or mix and match for variety.

4 | Alternatively, you can add single beads sparsely to make a circle or use the backstitch to fill in the entire outline of a circle. Try to space out the beads evenly around the circle for a neater look. Use the same-size beads for the whole circle or mix in a variety of shapes, sizes, and colors.

5 | Fill in some circles using a mix of beads and sequins. Simply add the beads or sequins one at a time to fill the center of the circle. Again, you can use the same size, shape, and color beads and sequins or vary them to add more texture and variety to the finished shawl.

Embroidered Shawl

Bead-Embroidered Table Runner

This personalized table runner can be beaded to match any décor or season. Use autumnal oranges, greens, and browns for one look or lime greens, hot pinks, and zingy yellows for another.

Skill level: INTERMEDIATE
Time: 15 hours

Bead-Embroidered Table Runner

Materials
- Store-bought plain cream table runner
- About 40 g size 11 seed beads in the colors of your choice
- Reel of cream beading or embroidery thread

Tools
- Scissors
- Needle
- Tools for transferring the design (see the Techniques section on page 44)

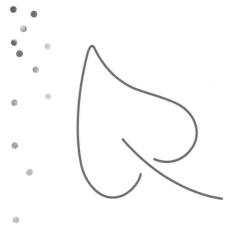

1 | Using any of the transfer techniques described in the Techniques section on page 44, transfer the leaf motif to the table runner. Here we used carbon paper to transfer the leaf motif on page 189. You can choose whether to bead the motifs simply around the edges or to cover the whole surface of the runner. Here we have beaded along the edges of the runner.

Bead-Embroidered Table Runner

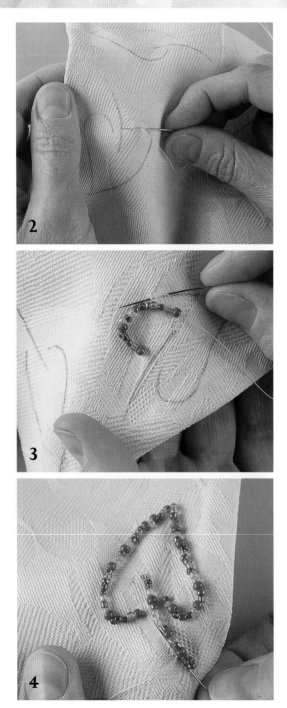

2 | Begin by threading the needle with some thread; then secure the thread to the work by weaving through the fabric to attach it and trim it as close as possible to the fabric so that it doesn't show. Be sure that the thread has been attached so you are in the correct position to start beading anywhere on one of the leaf motifs.

3 | Using the backstitch (see the Techniques section on page 47), bead around the leaf motif. Here we have used a selection of colored seed beads, but you could choose to make the leaf one color and the stem another. You could also choose to make each leaf a different color.

4 | When you have beaded the leaf stem, finish off the thread by weaving it through the fabric, underneath a line of beads in the motif, to hide the thread end completely.

Bead-Embroidered Table Runner

Bead-Encrusted Evening Bag

Create an interesting three-dimensional effect by attaching sequins on top of varying numbers of beads. The beading is worked on a length of wide ribbon and glued onto a ready-made evening bag.

Skill level: INTERMEDIATE
Time: 4 hours

Bead-Encrusted Evening Bag

Materials

- 1-in. (2.5-cm)-wide beige ribbon, 4 in. (10 cm) longer than width of bag
- 25 g size 11 silver, gold, and cream rocaille beads
- 25 g size 9 silver and gold rocaille beads
- 1 g 6-mm silver, gold, and mother-of-pearl sequins
- 1 g 8-mm silver, gold, and mother-of-pearl sequins
- 1 g 1-cm silver, gold, and mother-of-pearl sequins
- 2 g 8-mm gold bugle beads
- 2 g 5-mm bicone crystal beads
- Reel of gold beading thread
- Gold fabric evening bag
- Fabric glue

Tools

- #10 beading needle
- Glue spreader

1 | Press under ⅝ in. (1.5 cm) on one end of the ribbon. Bring the needle and thread to the right side of the ribbon at the pressed end. Thread on a 6-mm sequin, then a rocaille bead. Insert the needle back through the sequin into the ribbon and pull the thread so that the bead sits on the sequin.

2 | Bring the needle to the right side beside the sequin. To attach a sequin on top of a bugle bead, thread on a bugle bead, a sequin, then a rocaille bead. Insert the needle back through the sequin and bugle bead and into the ribbon. Pull the thread so that the bugle bead stands upright.

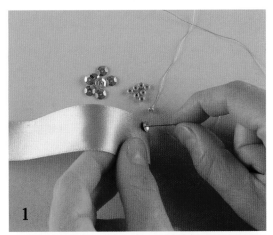

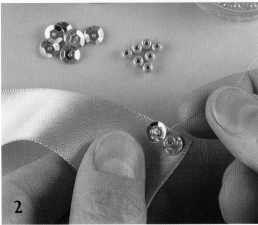

Bead-Encrusted Evening Bag

3 | To attach a bicone crystal bead, bring the needle to the right side and thread on a bicone bead, then a rocaille bead. Insert the needle back through the bicone bead into the ribbon and pull the thread so that the rocaille bead sits on the bicone bead.

4 | Attach a sequin by threading on 1, 2, or 3 rocaille beads, then the sequin and another rocaille bead. Insert the needle back through the sequin and all the beads except the last one.

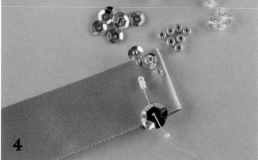

5 | Continue sewing sequins and beads to the ribbon, placing them side by side for even coverage. Check the length of the ribbon across the width of the handbag. When you are approximately 1½ in. (4 cm) from the extending end of the ribbon, mark the end of the handbag on the ribbon with a pin. Turn under the end of the ribbon at the pinned mark and cut off the extra ribbon ⅝ in. (1.5 cm) beyond the pinned mark. Bead to the end of the ribbon.

6 | Check the length of the beaded ribbon across the bag again and sew on more beads if necessary. Use a glue spreader to spread fabric glue sparingly on the back of the ribbon and glue it across the bag, making sure the top edge of the ribbon is ¾ in. (2 cm) below the upper edge.

Bead-Embroidered Lavender Sachet

This personalized lavender sachet will be a much-appreciated and treasured gift for whoever receives it. Make these as presents or just to treat yourself.

Skill level: INTERMEDIATE
Time: 4 hours

Bead-Embroidered Lavender Sachet

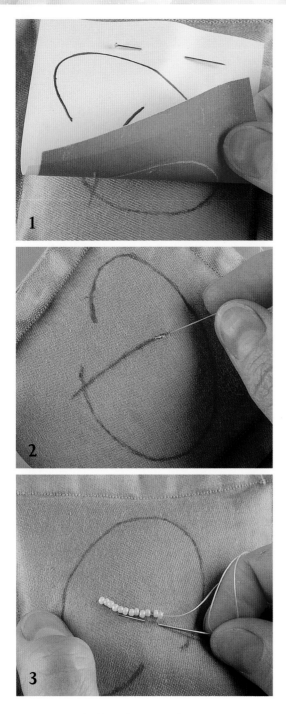

1

2

3

Materials
* Store-bought fabric lavender sachet
* About 10 g size 11 cream seed beads
* 1 g cream bugle beads
* Reel of white bead or embroidery thread

Tools
* Scissors
* #10 beading needle
* Tools for transferring the design (see the Techniques section on page 44)

1 | Using any of the transfer techniques described in the Techniques section on page 44, transfer your chosen initial (see templates on page 188) onto the sachet. Here, we used carbon paper to transfer the initial. Enlarge or reduce the initial on a photocopier if appropriate.

2 | After threading the needle with some white thread, secure the thread to the work by weaving through the fabric to attach it. Make sure the thread end is either hidden inside the sachet or trim it as close as possible to the fabric so that it doesn't show.

3 | Using the backstitch (see the Techniques section on page 47), carefully begin to bead over the lines of the initial.

Bead-Embroidered Lavender Sachet

4 | If you reach a section where one line crosses another, use either of the methods described in the Techniques section on page 48 to cross the lines. You can choose to either bead one line over another or, for a smoother, flatter finish, leave a gap the width of 1 bead where the lines cross over. Then bead into the gap.

5 | Use the seed beads and bugle beads to add some simple flower motifs to decorate the fabric. Some examples you may like to try:

- Sew on single bugle beads to represent the petals, adding a seed bead in the center.
- Pick up 2 or 3 seed beads at a time and sew them on in clusters to make petals—picking up more beads will make longer petals. Again, sew on another seed bead to make a center for the flower.
- You can also use a mix of bugle beads and seed beads to make the petals, adding a seed bead at either end of the bugle bead to make longer petals.

6 | Once the motifs are fully beaded, simply weave the thread through the fabric, underneath some beading, to secure and hide the end. When the thread is secured, trim as close to the work as possible to keep it looking neat.

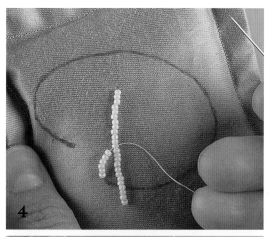

Flower-Embroidered Napkins

These pretty napkins will be sure to enhance any table. The simple flower and leaf motifs can be beaded to match or contrast with your décor or table setting.

Skill level: INTERMEDIATE
Time: 1 hour

Flower-Embroidered Napkins

Materials (per napkin)
- White napkin
- Reel of white beading or embroidery thread
- 1 pink sequin
- 2 g size 15 pink seed beads
- 1 g size 15 green beads

Tools
- Tools for transferring the design (see the Techniques section on page 44)
- Embroidery hoop (optional)
- #10 beading needle
- Scissors

1 | Using your choice of method for transferring designs (see the Techniques section on page 44), transfer the flower and leaf motif (see page 189) to one corner of your napkin. Here we've used tracing paper. You may prefer to work without the design and judge it by eye—the choice is yours.

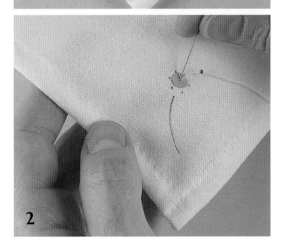

2 | Place the napkin into the embroidery hoop if you are using one; then take a length of thread and start the thread in the center of the flower. Pick up the sequin, then 1 pink seed bead, and pass the needle back through the hole of the sequin to attach it in place. This will be the center of the flower.

Flower-Embroidered Napkins

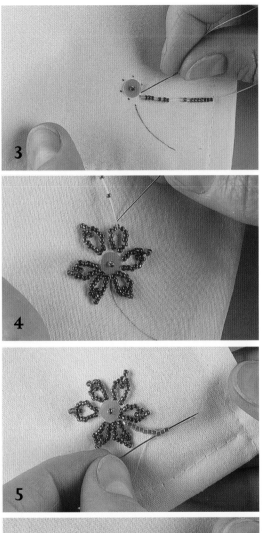

3 | Bring the needle up through one of the transferred dots to the side of the sequin and, using the chain stitch (see the Techniques section on page 49), bead a petal using the petal-color seed beads.

4 | Continue adding chain-stitch petals until you have beaded 6 petals around the sequin center.

5 | Using the backstitch (see the Techniques section on page 47), bead the flower's stem with the green seed beads. Start beading the stem at the flower end and bead down toward the base.

6 | At the end of the flower stem, use the chain stitch to add a leaf to the flower motif. Finish the thread off securely.

Variation

Flower napkin variations

You can bead the flower and leaf all in one color or, as shown above, leave the stem and leaf off for a different look. Why not bead a set of matching napkins or a set with the same flower and leaf motifs but in different color combinations? The possibilities are endless! It is all a matter of personal preference.

Wirework

Chandelier Earrings

These are full, big earrings that use chandelier posts from which to hang the beads. For maximum glamour, make the very full main project; for a slightly more conservative option, choose the alternative design.

Skill level: INTERMEDIATE
Time: 2 hours

Chandelier Earrings

Materials

- 1 bag Czech mixed beads in amber
- 1 bag Czech mixed beads in topaz
- 20 × 2-in. (5-cm) fancy Bali silver head pins
- 18 silver 2-in. (5-cm) head pins
- 2 silver Bali 5-hole chandelier posts
- 38 × ¼-in. (5-mm) silver jump rings
- 2 Bali silver earring posts

Tools

- Needle-nose pliers
- Round-nose pliers
- Wire cutters
- Crimpers
- 2 flat-nose pliers

1 | Tip out both packs of Czech beads and separate them into identical pairs of beads, one for each earring. Select 10 larger beads and 9 smaller ones for each pair.

2 | Thread the 20 larger beads onto the fancy Bali head pins and make a wrapped loop on all the beads (see the Techniques section on page 53). Do the same with the 18 smaller beads, threading them onto the silver head pins. Lay out the wrapped beads next to the chandelier posts where they will be hung, making sure there is a good mix of colors and bead sizes on all sides.

3 | Gently open the split loop inside the chandelier post with the round-nose pliers and hang the selected wrapped bead, then close the loop.

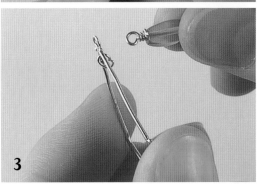

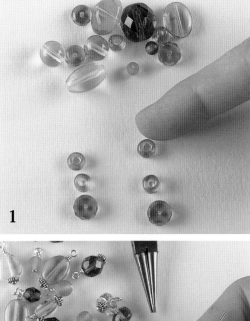

Chandelier Earrings

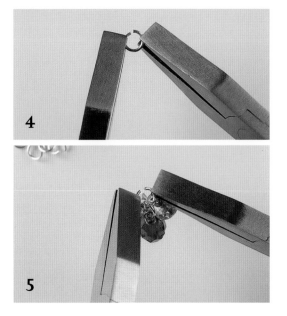

4 | Open 36 jump rings, using two pairs of flat-nose pliers (see Techniques section on page 54).

5 | To attach the beads, start with the center drop. Pick up 1 jump ring with the flat-nose pliers, thread on 2 large beads, and close. Pick up another jump ring, thread it through the previous jump ring, add 1 small and 1 large wrapped bead on either side, and close it. Pick up a third jump ring and do the same, attaching 1 small wrapped bead on either side again. Pick up a fourth jump ring, thread it through the previous jump ring, and close it. Repeat this with the fifth and sixth jump rings. Thread the seventh jump ring through the sixth jump ring, loop it through the middle hole at the base of the chandelier post, then close it. Use these techniques to complete the drops in the pattern set out below.

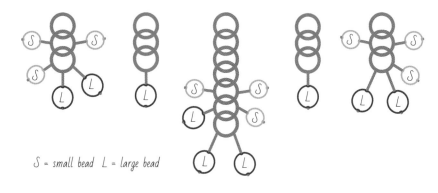

S = small bead   L = large bead

6 | When all the beads are attached, fit the earring post. To do this, open the earring post using the round-nose pliers, thread it through the loop at the top of the chandelier post, and close it.

Chandelier Earrings

S = small bead   L = large bead

Variation

Mini chandelier earrings

These earrings are smaller than the previous project and will suit those of you who prefer something less flamboyant. They are also a more suitable alternative for daytime wear, since they are lighter and more comfortable on the ears!

To make these earrings, you will need 14 jump rings, 12 large beads, and 6 small beads. Follow the diagram above, using the techniques described in the main project.

Charm Bracelet

A timeless classic that can be worn with just about anything, this bracelet is easily adaptable and can be made in whatever colors or style of beads you choose.

Skill level: BEGINNER
Time: 1 hour

Charm Bracelet

Materials

- 6 × 8-mm bicone crystal AB beads
- 6 × 6-mm silver melon-shaped beads
- 12 × 2-in. (5-cm) silver head pins
- 37 × 2-in. (5-cm) silver jump rings (18 closed and 19 open— see the Techniques section on page 54)
- 1 small silver toggle clasp

Tools

- Needle-nose pliers
- Round-nose pliers
- Wire cutters
- Crimping pliers
- 2 flat-nose pliers

1 | Thread each crystal and silver bead onto a head pin and make a wrapped loop (see the Techniques section on page 53).

2 | Pick up an open jump ring with the flat-nose pliers and thread on 1 crystal wrapped bead and 2 closed jump rings. Close the open jump ring with the help of the other flat-nose pliers (see the Techniques section on page 54).

3 | Lay the beads out flat so that you have the 2 empty jump rings on either side of the 1 ring with the crystal on it.

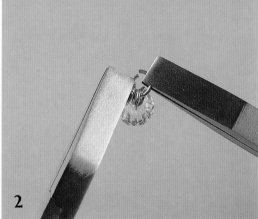

Charm Bracelet

4 | On the right-hand jump ring, add an open jump ring. On the open jump ring, thread on 1 wrapped silver bead and 1 closed jump ring. Lay the beads out flat to make sure that the wrapped silver bead is hanging on the same side of the chain as the crystal. Close the jump ring with the flat-nose pliers. Repeat this step, alternating the crystal and silver beads until you have no beads left.

5 | To finish off the bracelet on either side, continue to follow Step 4 but without threading on any beads until the bracelet is 1 in. (2.5 cm) smaller than the desired length. Make sure that either side of the charms has an equal number of jump rings.

6 | At either end, thread on half of the toggle clasp to the final open jump rings and then close to finish.

Charm Bracelet

Variation

Matching earrings

Why not team up your charm bracelet with matching earrings? These earrings are a simple variation of the bracelet.

Make a chain of 5 jump rings and thread on 1 silver wrapped bead. Make another chain of 7 jump rings and thread on 1 wrapped crystal bead. Thread the 2 top jump rings into the loop of the earring post.

Crystal Earrings

What to wear? The decision is so crystal clear. Perfect when worn in the daytime or evening, these shimmering crystals dangling from your ears will catch everybody's attention. A definite must-have for your jewelry collection. Quick and easy to make, you could have a set to match every outfit.

Skill level: BEGINNER
Time: 1 hour

Crystal Earrings

Materials

- 6 × 6-mm crystal beads (2 pale green, 2 yellow, 2 dark green)
- 4 × 5-mm crystal beads (2 olive green, 2 amber)
- 4 × 4-mm orange crystal beads
- 2 × 24 gauge 2-in. (5-cm) silver head pins
- 2 silver earring hooks

Tools

- Round-nose pliers
- Flat-nose pliers
- Wire cutters

1 | Place three (one of each color) 6-mm crystal beads on each head pin, followed by two (one of each color) 5-mm crystal beads, and finish with two 4-mm orange crystal beads.

2 | Create a turned loop on each head pin, as described in the Techniques section on page 52, using the flat-nose and round-nose pliers, but make sure not to close the loops completely at this stage.

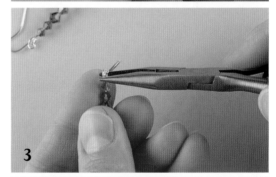

3 | Slip the turned loop onto the earring hook and close the loop using the flat-nose pliers. Repeat with the second earring.

Variation

Dangly earrings

You can use any sort of beads to make these earrings—be as bold and as daring as you like! Using the instructions for the basic dangling earrings, you can substitute the crystals for any type of beads.

Beaded Key Ring

A tactile beaded key ring that will liven up any set of keys. It can also be converted into a handbag charm by adding a large split ring instead of a key ring at the top.

Skill level: INTERMEDIATE
Time: 1 ½ hours

Beaded Key Ring

Materials

- 1 bag Czech mixed beads in amethyst
- 8 × 2-in. (5-cm) silver fancy Bali head pins
- 10 × 2-in. (5-cm) silver head pins
- 4 × 8-mm silver jump rings
- Key-ring head

Tools

- Needle-nose pliers
- Round-nose pliers
- Crimping pliers
- 2 flat-nose pliers
- Wire cutters

1 | Tip out the pack of Czech beads and sort them into 3 groups: large, medium, and small. Thread 8 large beads onto the fancy Bali head pins and make a wrapped loop on all the beads (see the Techniques section on page 53). Do the same with the 10 medium-sized beads, threading them onto the silver head pins. Reserve the smaller beads for another project.

2 | Open all the jump rings using the flat-nose pliers (see the Techniques section on page 54). Pick up 1 jump ring with the flat-nose pliers and randomly thread on 6 of the wrapped beads (3 large and 3 medium); then close the jump ring using both pairs of flat-nose pliers (see the Techniques section on page 54).

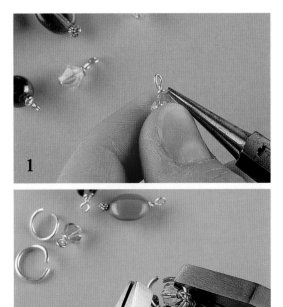

Beaded Key Ring

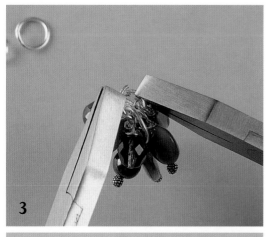

3 | Pick up another jump ring with the flat-nose pliers and thread on 3 wrapped beads. Now take the jump ring from Step 2 and thread it onto this open jump ring. Add 3 more wrapped beads and then close it using both pairs of flat-nose pliers. You should now have 2 connected jump rings with 6 wrapped beads on each.

4 | Repeat Step 3 so that you have 3 connected jump rings with 6 wrapped beads on each ring. Make sure that 3 beads fall to the left and 3 to the right on each of the last 2 rings.

5 | Pick up the fourth jump ring with the flat-nose pliers and thread it through the third jump ring and the loop at the bottom of the key ring. Close it using both pairs of flat-nose pliers.

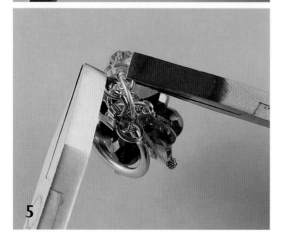

Beaded Key Ring

Variation
Long-strand key ring

This stunning variation is achieved by adding more wrapped beads per jump ring and making a longer strand before adding it to the key ring.

You could try making up your own design, varying the size, color, and style of the beads. You could also choose beads with a theme or try contrasting colors. This is a great way to use up spare large beads left over from other projects.

Spiral Ring and Charm Ring

These rings are open-ended so they can fit any finger size. If you don't have a ring dowel, you can use any cylindrical object that is ring size, such as a marker pen.

Skill level: INTERMEDIATE
Time: 1 hour

Spiral Ring and Charm Ring

Materials

For the spiral ring
* 6 ½ in. (16.5 cm) 16-gauge half-hard sterling silver wire

For the charm ring
* 6 × 6-mm round blue lace agate beads
* 6 × 6-mm round fire opal crystals
* 12 × 1-in. (2.5-cm) silver head pins

Tools
* Tape measure
* Ring dowel or equivalent
* Wire cutters
* File
* Nonpermanent marker pen
* Round-nose pliers
* Needle-nose pliers

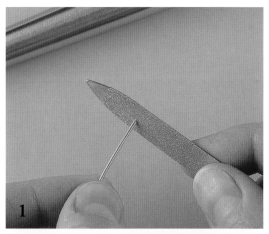

1 | To make the spiral ring, measure the circumference of the dowel and add 4 in. (10 cm) to this length. Cut a piece of wire to this size and file the ends of the wire smooth (see the Techniques section on page 51).

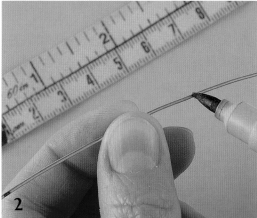

2 | Measure 2 in. (5 cm) in from either end of the wire and mark with a nonpermanent marker pen.

3 | To start the spiral, use the round-nose pliers and form a loop at one end of the wire. Hold the loop in the flat-nose pliers and continue to spiral until it meets the mark made in Step 2. Repeat on the other end of the wire, this time spiraling in the opposite direction.

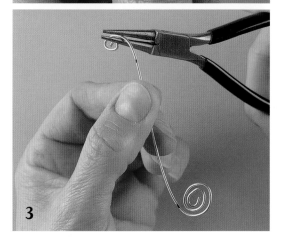

Spiral Ring and Charm Ring

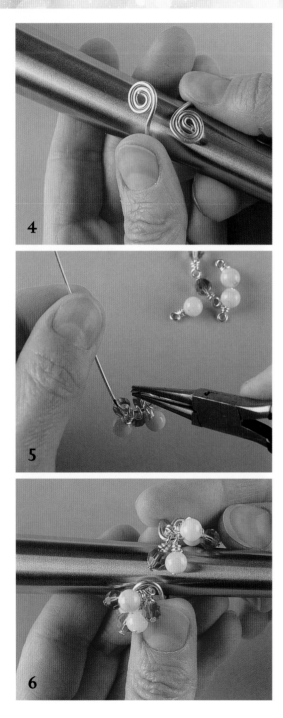

4

5

6

Crafter's Tip

To prevent the flat-nose pliers from marking the silver wire, wrap the tip of the pliers in masking tape.

4 | Hold one end of the wire against the dowel and gently bend it around until it forms a ring shape.

5 | For the charm variation, repeat Steps 1 and 2, but add 1½ in. (4 cm) to the circumference of the dowel before cutting the wire to size. Measure and mark ¾ in. (2 cm) in from either end of the wire. Thread all the beads onto the silver head pins and make a wrapped loop on all the beads (see the Techniques section on page 53). Hold one end of the wire in the round-nose pliers and gently form a U-shape, bending back toward the wire. Stop just before the end meets the wire. Thread on 6 of the wire-wrapped beads so that they rest in the U-bend. Pick up the end of the wire in the round-nose pliers and continue to bend until it reaches the mark made. Repeat on the other end of the wire, bending in the opposite direction.

6 | To finish, repeat Step 4 to form the ring shape.

Variation

Colorful charm rings

The blue charm ring shows just how different this ring can look by adding more charms in Step 5.

Flower Bobby Pin, Comb, and Barrette

Once you learn to make the lovely beaded flower, you can take your pick of which hair accessory you'd like to make. There are three possibilities, so try your hand at one or all three! They make a great-looking set.

Skill level: INTERMEDIATE
Time: 3 hours for all 3 accessories

Flower Bobby Pin, Comb, and Barrette

Materials
For each flower
- 6 × 7-mm pink rice-shaped fairy luster beads, for the petals
- 6 size 11 white luster seed beads, for the tips of the petals
- 1 × 6-mm round rose alabaster crystal bead, for the center of the flower
- 26-in. (65-cm) 28-gauge soft silver wire

Tools
- Needle-nose pliers
- Wire cutters

TO MAKE THE FLOWER

1 | Thread 1 rice bead and 1 seed bead onto the wire. Leave a tail of 6 in. (15 cm) below the rice bead and thread the other end of the wire back through the rice bead and pull tight, using the needle-nose pliers.

2 | Thread another rice bead and seed bead onto the longer end of the wire and push up close to the first set of beads. Thread the wire back up through the rice bead and pull tight. Continue to do this until you have 6 sets of beads.

3 | Pinch both ends of the wire and twist together twice, using your fingers.

4 | Fold over the longer end of wire up to the other side of the flower shape. Thread on the 6-mm round rose alabaster crystal and bring the wire back down the opposite side of the flower. Twist both ends of wire together twice. **Do not** cut any excess wire at this stage. You now have one complete flower.

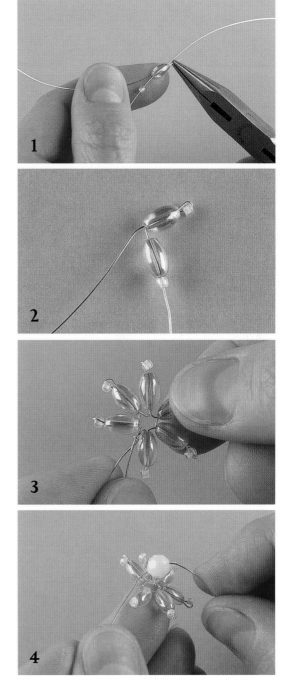

Flower Bobby Pin, Comb, and Barrette

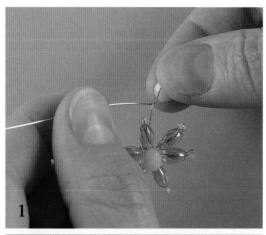

Materials

For the bobby pin

- 1 bobby pin
- 1 flower (see page 167)
- 2 × 6-mm round rose alabaster crystal beads, for the petal extensions
- 2 × 4-mm bicone light rose AB crystal beads, for the petal extensions

TO MAKE THE BOBBY PIN

1 | Make a flower (see Steps 1 to 4 on page 167). Thread a 4-mm bicone light rose AB crystal onto the longer end of wire and position it ½ in. (1.5 cm) from the flower. Holding the crystal between your finger and thumb, fold the wire back to the center of the flower and hold it in place with your other thumb. Twist the wires clockwise until they are fully twisted together. Repeat this 4 more times, alternating between the round rose alabaster crystals and the 4-mm bicone light rose AB crystals, and spread the twisted wires in a fan around one side of the flower.

2 | Place the loop of the bobby pin directly under the wire and wrap the 2 wires separately in opposite directions around the grip, about 10 times each. Cut off the excess wire with wire cutters and manipulate the flower into shape.

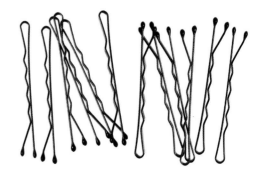

Flower Bobby Pin, Comb, and Barrette

Materials
For the hair comb
* 3 flowers (see page 167)
* 1 × 3¼-in. (8-cm) hair comb
* 12 × 6-mm crystal matte fire-polished Czech pressed beads
* 12 × 6-mm crystal silver-lined fire-polished Czech pressed beads
* 3 × 39-in. (1-m) lengths 28-gauge silver soft wire

TO MAKE THE HAIR COMB

1 | Take the 3 lengths of wire loop and hook them around the last tooth of the comb; then twist all 3 pieces together twice, leaving a 4-in. (10-cm) tail.

2 | Take two of the long pieces of wire and thread them over the front of the bar and between the first and second teeth. Bring the 2 wires back out at the side of the bar and pull tight. Thread 12 fire-polished beads, alternating the colors onto these 2 wires.

3 | Trim the 4-in. (10-cm) tails from Step 1 down to 1 in. (2.5 cm) with the wire cutters, and press them flat against the front of the comb, above the teeth. Bring the 2 beaded lengths of wire over these tails and flat across the top of the comb.

4 | Bring the wire without beads around the back, between the first and second teeth of the comb, then between the first and second beads of each row. Wrap the wire around the back of the comb and bring it up through the next tooth. Do this all the way across the comb. You may need to miss a few teeth while wrapping to keep the beads tight.

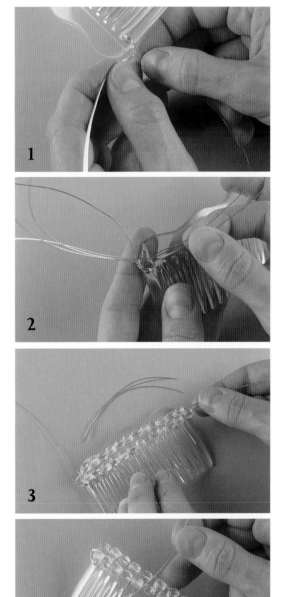

Flower Bobby Pin, Comb, and Barrette

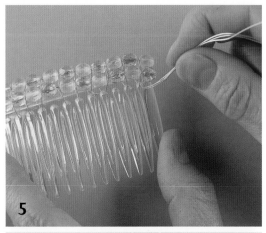

5 | When you reach the end of the comb, twist all 3 ends of wire together and wrap them through the last tooth of the comb, around the back and up and over, going underneath the beaded wires. Pull them tight; then loop the wires under the beaded wires twice more and trim the excess wire with the wire cutters.

6 | Make 3 flowers (see Steps 1 to 4 on page 167). Position 1 flower on the center of the bar and wrap the 2 wires separately: one clockwise and the other counterclockwise around the wire, holding the beads in place. Repeat 5 times; then trim the excess wire with the wire cutters.

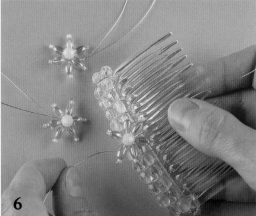

7 | Repeat with the two other flowers placed on either side of the center flower, and press the flowers into place and, if necessary, into shape. Make sure no sharp wires stick out: Either trim the ends with wire cutters or push them into the comb underneath the beads.

Flower Bobby Pin, Comb, and Barrette

Materials

For the barrette

* 3 flowers (see page 167)
* 1 barrette
* 12 × 6-mm crystal matte fire-polished Czech pressed beads
* 12 × 6-mm crystal silver-lined fire-polished Czech pressed beads
* 3 × 39-in. (1-m) lengths 28-gauge silver soft wire

TO MAKE THE BARRETTE

The instructions for the barrette are the same as for the comb, but instead of wrapping the wires around the teeth of the comb, you wrap them around the base of the barrette.

Decorated Candle

This is a really simple way to make a beautiful beaded candle. It is so easy that you'll have no problems progressing onto your own designs.

Skill level: INTERMEDIATE
Time: 5 hours

Decorated Candle

Materials
- 8½ × 11-in. (A4) sheet tissue paper
- 1 white candle— height: 7 in. (18 cm); diameter: 3¼ in. (8 cm)
- 503 × 1-in. (2.5-cm) silver head pins
- 24 × 6-mm bicone violet beads
- 194 × 4-mm violet AB fire-polished Czech beads
- 122 × 6-mm violet AB fire-polished Czech beads
- 37 × 8-mm amethyst fire-polished Czech beads
- 126 × 4-mm crystal AB fire-polished Czech beads

Tools
- 5 felt-tip pens in assorted colors
- Ruler
- Scissors
- Wire cutters

1 | Photocopy the candle template on page 187. Place the sheet of tissue paper over the template and, using a different-colored felt-tip pen for each different bead color/size, mark a dot in the center of the crosses on the design. This is where each head pin will be inserted. Also draw onto the tissue paper the outline of the template; then cut it out.

Decorated Candle

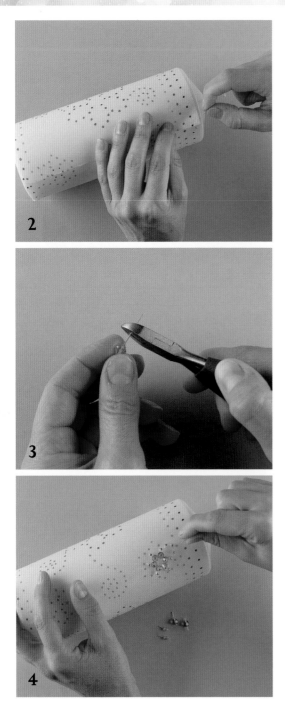

2 | Wrap the tissue paper around the candle so that the half flowers at either end of the paper meet to form full flowers. Attach the tissue paper using a head pin cut down to ½ in. (1 cm) in each of the 4 corners. The head pin should not go all the way into the candle, but should be inserted just far enough to keep the tissue paper in place.

3 | Select the bead color/size with which you wish to start. It is easier to start on the smaller shapes and work out. Thread 1 bead onto 1 head pin and cut off the excess with wire cutters so that there is ⅜ in. (7 mm) of head pin sticking out of the bead.

4 | Push the head pin into the candle where marked on the tissue paper. The head pin should be pushed in so securely that the bead does not move. Repeat this process until all the marks made on the tissue paper have the corresponding beads added.

Decorated Candle

5 | Remove the corner head pins from Step 2, keeping the tissue paper in place. Very carefully tear away the tissue paper from the candle. You may need to hold the beads and head pins in place when doing this. If any come loose, just push them back in so that they are once again secure. This step can be a bit tricky to execute, but once you see the finished candle, you will know it was well worth the effort.

Variation

Star-studded candle

To make this beautiful star-studded candle, you will need 274 × 1-in. (2.5-cm) silver head pins and 270 × 6-mm clear bicone Swarovski crystals AB. Photocopy the candle template on page 186 and follow the instructions in the main project to complete the candle.

Beaded Lamp Shade

This project shows how to bead on a store-bought metal lamp-shade frame. This project was worked on a drum-shaped frame, but many frame shapes and sizes are available. Glass beads work really well with this type of project because when the lamp is switched on, the light shines beautifully through the beads.

Skill level: ADVANCED
Time: 12 hours

Beaded Lamp Shade

Materials

- 71 ft. (21 m) 24-gauge silver wire
- 1 drum-shaped metal lamp-shade frame—height: 5 in. (12.5 cm); circumference: 18 in. (46 cm)
- 84 × 8-mm Indian round glass beads—cobalt
- 132 × 8-mm Indian round glass beads—sapphire
- 132 × 8-mm Indian round glass beads—aqua
- 132 × 8-mm Indian round glass beads—teal
- 84 × 8-mm Indian round glass beads—crystal
- 318 × 4-mm Indian round glass beads—crystal

Tools

- Needle-nose pliers
- Wire cutters
- Flat-nose pliers

1 | Cut a length of wire approximately 39 in. (1 m) long, using the wire cutters. With the needle-nose pliers, wrap one end 3 times around the top of the circular frame very near to one of the vertical struts, bringing the wire toward you. Continue wrapping, but bring the wire down the vertical strut and wrap 5 times counterclockwise. Grip the wire with the pliers and pull to check that it is secure and tight. Always tighten each wrap with the flat-nose pliers because this will give a good tension to your work.

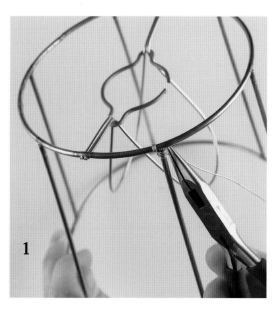

Beaded Lamp Shade

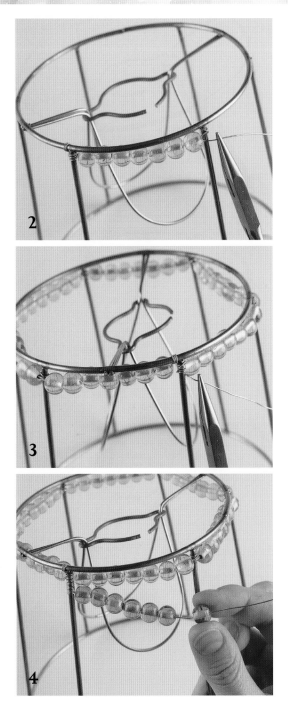

2 | Thread on 7 colored beads and pull the wire taught. Lay the wire over the vertical strut to the right of the one you started on and take the wire behind and around, bringing it out above the beaded wire. Take the wire around again and bring it out below.

3 | Work your way around the frame until you come back to where you started. Wrap the wire over the previous wire and around the strut, bringing the wire out above the initial wrapping. Then wrap again around the strut and bring the wire out below. Wrap the wire around the strut 10 more times.

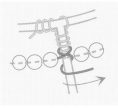

4 | Repeat Steps 2 and 3 until you have covered the entire frame. When you run out of one length of wire, wrap the end securely around the nearest vertical strut. Do the same to add the new piece of wire. If possible, go under and over the other wires for added security.

Beaded Lamp Shade

5 | When the whole frame is complete, you will need to cover the vertical struts with the smaller beads to hide the unsightly wire. To do this, wrap a 12-in. (30-cm) piece of wire around the top circular frame of the lamp shade. Thread on 28 × 4-mm crystal beads and pull flat with the strut. Wrap the wire on either side of the strut on the bottom of the circular frame.

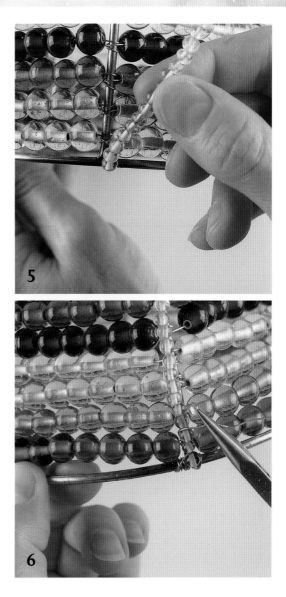

6 | Wrap a new piece of wire about 39 in. (1 m) in length at the same place as where the previous wire ended on the bottom, and bring it over the top of the first small bead, around the back, and back up 2 beads along. Do this all the way up/down the strut. This anchors the wire with the beads on it in place. Do this for all 6 struts.

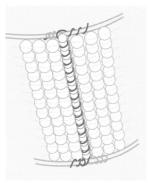

Beaded Lamp Shade

7 | To bead the circular top and bottom of the frame, use the same technique as on the struts. Wrap on a length of wire 1½ times the circumference of the frame. Thread on as many 4-mm beads as it takes to go all the way around the outside of the circular frame and remove the last bead. To secure this wire in place, wrap on another length of wire and bring it over the top and between the first and second beads, under and back around 2 beads along. Both lengths of wire should start and finish in the same place. Continue until you have covered the frame of the base. Once the frame is complete, carefully check the frame for any ends of wire that are sticking out and flatten them to the base with the flat-nose pliers.

Beaded Lamp Shade

Suppliers

IN THE UNITED STATES

BEADWORKS INTERNATIONAL, INC.
139 Washington Street
Norwalk, CT 06854
www.beadworks.com

JEWELRY SUPPLY, INC.
301 Derek Place
Roseville, CA 95678
www.jewelrysupply.com

METALLIFEROUS, INC.
34 West 46th Street, 3rd Floor
New York, NY 10036
www.metalliferous.com

IN CANADA

CANADA BEADING SUPPLY
8B–190 Colonnade Road South
Ottawa, ON K2E 7J5
www.canbead.com

THAT BEAD LADY
390 Davis Drive, Unit 103
Newmarket, ON L3Y 7T8
OR
175 Crossland Gate
Newmarket, ON L3X 1A7
www.thatbeadlady.com

IN AUSTRALIA

AUSTRALIAN CRAFT NETWORK
P.O. Box 153
Kings Langley, NSW 2147
www.auscraftnet.com.au

CRAFT.ONTHEINTERNET.COM.AU
53a High Street, Taree
P.O. Box 525
Matraville, NSW 2036
www.craft.ontheinternet.com.au

SPACETRADER
P.O. Box 1019
St. Kilda South
Melbourne, VIC 3182
www.spacetrader.com.au

OZ BEADS
www.ozbeads.com.au

UNIQUE BEADS
22 Arcadia Road
Glebe, NSW 2037
www.uniquebeads.com.au

IN NEW ZEALAND

BEADZ UNLIMITED
Upstairs Galleria of Christchurch
7 New Regent Street
Central City
Christchurch
www.beadzunlimited.com

Templates

Big Book of Weekend Beading

candle (page 176)

Decorated candle (page 172)

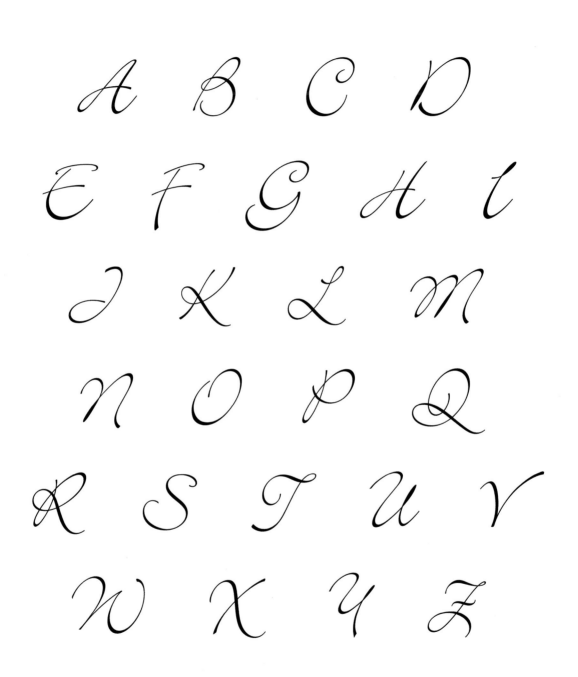

Bead-embroidered lavender sachet (page 139)

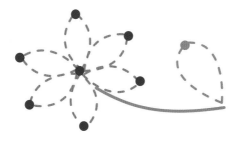

Flower-embroidered napkins (page 142)

Bead-embroidered table runner (page 132)

Index

Photo Credits

Photo Credits

About the Beading Designers

Jean Power, a prize-winning beader, teaches workshops, publishes patterns, and runs a beading and jewelry kit business. She is an expert in all aspects of beading and jewelry making, including wirework, chain maille, and bead embroidery. Visit her at *www.jeanpower.com.*

Natalie Cotgrove designs intricate wirework jewelry using crystals and semiprecious stones.

Julie Smallwood works primarily with sterling silver wire and crystals to create original, free-form pieces for special occasions and weddings.

Umbreen Hafeez enjoys beading in her spare time and loves to create one-off, unusual pieces of jewelry.

Cheryl Owen, author of *The Bead Jewelry Maker*, was a beader for a top London fashion house.